SOURCES OF OUR FAITH

SOURCES OF OUR FAITH

Inspirational Readings

KATHLEEN ROLENZ, EDITOR

SKINNER HOUSE BOOKS
BOSTON

www.skinnerhouse.org

Printed in the United States

Cover and text design by Suzanne Morgan

print ISBN: 978-1-55896-678-9
eBook ISBN: 978-1-55896-679-6

6 5 4 3 2
19 18 17 16

Permission acknowledgments begin on page 165.

Note: The Unitarian Universalist Association is committed to using gender-inclusive language. Where adaptations could not be made without unduly distorting flow and readability or violating copyright, we have presented quoted matter in its original form.

Every effort has been made to obtain permission to include each of these pieces. In some cases the author is deceased and we have been unable to locate her/his estate.

Library of Congress Cataloging-in-Publication Data

Sources of our faith : inspirational readings / Kathleen Rolenz, editor.
    p. cm.
 Includes bibliographical references and index.
 ISBN 978-1-55896-678-9 (pbk. : alk. paper)—ISBN 978-1-55896-679-6 (ebook)
1. Unitarian Universalist Association. I. Rolenz, Kathleen.
 BX9841.3.S69 2012
 289.1'32—dc23
                          2012011023

Dedicated to the original authors of our Sources—
Unitarian Universalists who drew from within the deep wells
of our faith, giving shape to this living tradition;

and to my husband, the Reverend Wayne Arnason—
my source of great joy.

SOURCES OF OUR FAITH

The living tradition we share draws from many sources:

1   Direct experience of that transcending mystery and wonder, affirmed in all cultures, which moves us to a renewal of the spirit and an openness to the forces which create and uphold life;

2   Words and deeds of prophetic women and men which challenge us to confront powers and structures of evil with justice, compassion, and the transforming power of love;

3   Wisdom from the world's religions which inspires us in our ethical and spiritual life;

4   Jewish and Christian teachings which call us to respond to God's love by loving our neighbors as ourselves;

5   Humanist teachings which counsel us to heed the guidance of reason and the results of science, and warn us against idolatries of the mind and spirit;

6   Spiritual teachings of Earth-centered traditions which celebrate the sacred circle of life and instruct us to live in harmony with the rhythms of nature.

CONTENTS

INTRODUCTION

The living tradition we share draws from many sources . . .

For over two hundred years Unitarians, Universalists, and Unitarian Universalists have been dancing with the Holy. At times, it seems as if our rational minds take the lead, moving us gracefully around the floor to the finely metered rhythms of a Bach gavotte. At other times, mystery and wonder lead the dance, where the steps are being revealed to us even as we dance them. Throughout history, we have moved to the rhythms of mystery and wonder, prophecy, wisdom, teachings from ancient and modern sources, and nature herself. These themes comprise the Sources from which we draw strength and support.

Think of the readings in this book as part of the musical score that undergirds Unitarian Universalism. This collection, I hope, represents the aspirations of the six Sources of Unitarian Universalism—the second half of the Purposes and Principles document.

Ours will always be a "living tradition," reflecting the ever-flowing stream of human thought and spirituality. The Sources outline the diversity of religious experience that forms the basis of Unitarian Universalist faith. Our tradition is held together by our profound respect and love for these teachings and inspirations. The Sources are the ideas and deeds that reflect human experience, but they also point to that which lies beyond human understanding. They remind us that first and foremost, Unitarian Universalism is a religion rooted in the experience of the holy. They serve as a guide in determining what is valid, deep, and meaningful about living.

I hope that the readings offered here will provide a refreshing insight into each of the Sources, and show why they are so vital to renewing this tradition from generation to generation. I have been influenced by the discipline of memorizing texts until they become an embodied part of my devotional practice. I invite you to use these quotations as part of a similar daily spiritual discipline. I hope the collection will also be valuable for anyone wishing to deepen their appreciation of the Sources through focused or occasional reading of the texts, either personally or in worship.

In the Christian practice known as *Lectio Divina,* readers engage with scripture through a four-step process: (1) Read the text, (2) Reflect on the text, (3) Respond to the text through writing or discussion, and (4) Rest, or simply sit with the text. You may find this structure helpful with these readings as well.

Another way to use this book could be as a six-day-a-week morning practice, to match the six Sources. On the seventh day, we don't rest—we go to church! Try selecting a reading from one of the Sources on the same day each week, or vary the order. You might live with one text from one Source for one week, then go on to another the next week, through a six-week cycle. You can use the readings as a thought for the day, or as a text to work on over time, committing it to memory. I look forward to hearing about other ways people might use this book as well.

These readings may also help those seeking to bring a more multicultural perspective to worship services. However, I counsel caution when using wisdom teachings from cultures and faiths not represented among us and with which we are not engaged. Unitarian Universalism draws from diverse sources; yet when we take sacred words out of context and give them new meanings, we may devalue and disrespect those from whom we borrow. As you use these readings in worship, I encourage you to contextualize them by describing the author's cultural context and the depth of meaning a reading or song can hold for those inside its culture of origin. See the Note on Multicultural Readings at the back of this book for ways to research online some of the cultures represented by the readings.

In the end, we cannot speak or write about the Sources without acknowledging the One Source that runs underneath them all—love. As our living tradition continues to unfold, opening us to new revelations of truth, love will guide us. And so we continue our dance with the Holy, our partner and Great Mystery, in our ongoing journey toward connection.

KATHLEEN ROLENZ

FIRST SOURCE

—◦—

*Direct experience of that transcending
mystery and wonder, affirmed in all
cultures, which moves us to a renewal
of the spirit and an openness to the
forces which create and uphold life*

MOSES ENCOUNTERED a Burning Bush and took off his shoes to honor the sacred ground he stood upon. Buddha saw the morning star and attained enlightenment. Muhammad rose from his sleep and recorded what he heard Allah telling him to write. Jesus fasted in the desert for forty days and then returned, full of the spirit, to preach about the kingdom of God. Each of these holy men pointed toward something larger than his own personal experience or our common existence. The first Source describes how we also point to our personal experiences of awe, trying not to mistake the pointing finger for the moon.

Direct experience has always been critical to the Unitarian Universalist understanding of religion. It has led us to become and to affirm heretics—those who courageously stand up to orthodoxy because they trust their own experience more than traditional authority.

Today, Unitarian Universalists recognize the influences of nineteenth-century Transcendentalists, who brought their bodies to the shore of Walden Pond, and their eyes to the New England woods around them. We have transcendent experiences of mystery and wonder in music, poetry and essays, in both public and private settings. We have them while sitting in the early morning hours with words that inspire us, or in the silent hush of a congregation in prayer, or through the joyous winding of a spiral dance. These experiences lift us out of ourselves and inspire us towards greater acts of courageous love. We find inspiration in the natural world—in the sly smile of a coyote in our backyard, the persistent unfurling of ferns in the spring, the dappled leaf and loamy smell of soil. We have these experiences and realize that they know no creeds and have no bounds.

In the beginning — silence
In the beginning — wonder
In the beginning — beauty
In the beginning — death. . . .

Holy the mystery; holy the journey;
Holy the hour of prayer.
Blessed and merciful; blessed and generous;
Sacred as simple air. . . .

Summoning duty, touch of compassion,
Keeper of song and flame;
Struggle and silence, praise and thanksgiving,
Truth beyond every name

In the beginning — on the horizon — Life!

KENDYL GIBBONS

Let us worship with our eyes and ears and fingertips; let us love the world through heart and mind and body.

KENNETH PATTON

Meister Eckhart wrote, "As thou art in church or cell, that same frame of mind carry out into the world, into its turmoil and its fitfulness." Deep within us all there is an amazing inner sanctuary of the soul, a holy place, a Divine Center, a speaking Voice, to which we may continuously return. Eternity is at our hearts, pressing upon our time-torn lives, warming us with intimations of an astounding destiny, calling us home unto Itself.

THOMAS KELLY

Behold! In the creation
Of the heavens and the earth;
In the alternation of the Night and the Day . . .
In the beasts of all kinds
That He scatters
Through the earth. . . .
(Here) indeed are Signs
For a people that are wise.

QUR'AN 2:164

Our life is an apprenticeship to the truth that around every circle another can be drawn; that there is no end in nature but every end is a beginning . . . and under every deep a lower deep opens.

RALPH WALDO EMERSON

For simple things that are not simple at all
For miracles of the common way . . .
    Sunrise . . . Sunset,
    Seedtime . . . Harvest,
    Hope . . . Joy . . . Ecstasy
For grace that turns
    our intentions into deeds
    our compassion into helpfulness
    our pain into mercy
For providence that
    sustains and supports our needs
We lift our hearts in thankfulness,
    and pray only to be more aware
and thus more alive.

GORDON B. MCKEEMAN

If you bring forth what is within you, what you bring forth will save you.
If you do not bring forth what is within you, what you do not bring forth will destroy you.

GOSPEL OF THOMAS, 70

If you cannot go into the desert, you must nonetheless "make some desert" in your life. Every now and then leaving . . . and looking for solitude to restore, in prolonged silence and prayer, the stuff of your soul.

CARLO CARRETTO

God called to him out of the bush, "Moses, Moses!" And he said, "Here I am." Then he said, "Come no closer! Remove the sandals from your feet, for the place on which you are standing is holy ground."

EXODUS 3:4–5

I like to walk alone on country paths, rice plants and wild grasses on both sides, putting each foot down on the earth in mindfulness, knowing that I walk on the wondrous earth. In such moments, existence is a miraculous and mysterious reality. People usually consider walking on water or in thin air a miracle. But I think the real miracle is not to walk either on water or in thin air, but to walk on earth. Every day we are engaged in a miracle which we don't even recognize: a blue sky, white clouds, green leaves, the black, curious eyes of a child—our own two eyes. All is a miracle.

THICH NHAT HANH

In the evening I went into the church-yard; the moon sailed above the rosy clouds. That crescent moon rose above the heavenward-pointing spire. At that hour a vision came upon my soul, whose final scene last month interpreted. The rosy clouds of illusion are all vanished, the moon has waxed to full. May my life be a church, full of devout thoughts, and solemn music.

MARGARET FULLER

I love the dark hours of my being.
My mind deepens into them.
There I can find, as in old letters,
the days of my life, already lived,
and held like a legend, and understood.

Then the knowing comes: I can open
to another life that's wide and timeless.

So I am sometimes like a tree
rustling over a gravesite
and making real the dream
of the one its living roots
embrace:

a dream once lost
among sorrows and songs.

RAINER MARIA RILKE

My spiritual practice consists of this: I think back on the events of the day and ask the question, "Where was God in this day?" It's a question that can be asked in a dozen different theological voices, and if God language fails to resonate, then we might ask merely, "Where today did I really hear the language of my life?" The question puts a sheen of attentiveness and care on even the most mundane dimensions of the day. It gives us a way to cradle the moments of a day just lived and see them again before they're too far away, to notice the regrets and failings as well as the joys.

KATHLEEN MCTIGUE

This morning, outside I stood
And saw a little red-winged bird
Shining like a burning bush
Singing like a scripture verse
It made me want to bow my head
I remember when church let out
How things have changed since then
Everything is holy now
It used to be a world half-there
Heaven's second rate hand-me-down
But I walk it with a reverent air
'Cause everything is holy now

PETER MAYER

I prefer the modest joys, the understated incarnations, the distilled moments of simple pleasure that are sneaky blessings to everyone:

the capacity to play and to be renewed by a restful sleep, the whole range of tastes from sweet to bitter and the mysteries in between, the delicate slender fingers of an infant child, the color of sky and sea and the vast complex of hues that melt through the eyes, the sheer wonder of sound shaking the inner soul with tones of depths and heights, the tender remembrance of times that were good and whole, the rustic places that lunged out and lodged in the heart, the persons who shared their secret loves in moments beyond all measuring, the coming of day and the sureness of the return of night, the loyalty of a pet when humans forget to care, the aloneness of solitude that stirs the mind in new directions, the muted meanings that each of us finds in the cycle of life and that hold fast through the fearful rhythms, and all of the subtle and lumbering awarenesses that pulse in us—

for which our hearts sing their joyful "Amen!"

DAVID RANKIN

Glory be to God for dappled things—
    For skies of couple-colour as a brinded cow;
        For rose-moles all in stipple upon trout that swim;
Fresh-firecoal chestnut-falls; finches' wings;
    Landscape plotted and pieced—fold, fallow, and plough;
        And all trades, their gear and tackle and trim.

All things counter, original, spare, strange;
    Whatever is fickle, freckled (who knows how?)
        With swift, slow; sweet, sour; adazzle, dim;
He fathers-forth whose beauty is past change:
            Praise him.

GERARD MANLY HOPKINS

If you could understand a single grain of wheat, you would die of wonder.

MARTIN LUTHER

There are mysteries which you can solve by taking thought. For instance a murder-mystery whose mysteriousness must be dispelled in order for the truth to be known. There are other mysteries which do not conceal a truth to think your way to, but whose truth is itself the mystery. The mystery of your self, for example. The more you try to fathom it, the more fathomless it is revealed to be. No matter how much of your self you are able to objectify and examine, the quintessential, living part of yourself will always elude you, i.e., the part that is conducting the examination. Thus you do not solve the mystery, you live the mystery. And you do that not by fully knowing yourself but by fully being yourself. To say that God is a mystery is to say that you can never nail him down. Even on Christ the nails proved ultimately ineffective.

FREDERICK BUECHNER

There is a life-force within your soul, seek that life.
There is a gem in the mountain of your body, seek that mine.
O traveler, if you are in search of That
Don't look outside, look inside yourself and seek That.

RUMI

"Miracles have ceased." Have they indeed? When? They had not ceased this afternoon when I walked into the wood and got into bright, miraculous sunshine in shelter from the roaring wind. Who sees a pine-cone, or the turpentine exuding from the tree, or a leaf, the unit of vegetation, fall from its bough as if it said, "The year is finished," or hears in the quiet piney glen the Chickadee chirping his cheerful note, or walks along the leafy promontory-like ridges which like natural causeways traverse the morass, or gazes upward at the rushing clouds, or downward at a moss or a stone and says to himself, "Miracles have ceased"?

RALPH WALDO EMERSON

All around us lies what we neither understand nor use. Our capacities, our instincts for this our present sphere are but half developed. Let us confine ourselves to that till the lesson be learned; let us be completely natural; before we trouble ourselves with the supernatural. I never see any of these things but I long to get away and lie under a green tree and let the wind blow on me. There is marvel and charm enough in that for me.

MARGARET FULLER

Were I to teach a course on God
I would begin with a plate of persimmons—
the sweet, crisp kind, the ones more
orange than red: the hard, squat Fuyus
I eat each November morning on hot
wheat cereal with almonds.

NANCY SHAFFER

I believe that one is converted when first one hears the low, vast murmur of life, of human life, troubling one's hitherto unconscious self. I believe one is born first unto oneself—for the happy developing of oneself, while the world is a nursery, and the pretty things are to be snatched for, and pleasant things tasted; some people seem to exist thus right to the end. But most are born to humanity, to a consciousness of all the laughing, and the never-ceasing murmur of pain and sorrow that comes from the terrible multitudes of brothers and sisters. Then, it appears to me, one gradually formulates one's religion, be it what it may. A person has no religion who has not slowly and painfully gathered one together, adding to it, shaping it; and one's religion is never complete and final, it seems, but must always be undergoing modification.

D.H. LAWRENCE, ADAPTED

The beauty of life is such that it will not let us go until we have offered the blessing we have to give. So let the beauty we have seen become the good that we do, and let us not wrest ourselves free from the claim that life places upon us until we, in faith with all those who have gone before us, place ourselves among those who bless the world.

Rebecca Parker

Today we are not dependent upon any text or the letter of any book. It is the spirit that giveth life and the spirit speaks to our souls.

Olympia Brown

What if there were a universe in which a world was born out of a smallish star, and into that world (at some point) flew red-winged blackbirds, and into it swam sperm whales, and into it bloomed crocuses, and into it blew wind to lift the tiniest hairs on naked arms in spring, and into it at some point grew onions, out of soil, and in went Mt. Everest and also the coyote we've spotted in the woods about a mile from here, just after sunrise on these mornings when the moon is full? (The very scent of him makes his brother, our dog, insane with fear and joy and ancient inbred memory.) Into that world came animals and elements and plants, and imagination, the mind and the

15

mind's eye. If such a universe existed and you noticed it, what would you do? What song would come out of your mouth, what prayer, what praises, what sacred offering, what whirling dance, what religion and what reverential gesture would you make to greet that world, every single day that you were in it?

VICTORIA SAFFORD

Is it beyond thee to be glad with the gladness of this rhythm? To be tossed and lost and broken in the whirl of this fearful joy? All things rush on, they stop not, they look not behind, no power can hold them back, they rush on.

Keeping steps with that restless, rapid music, seasons come dancing and pass away—colors, tunes, and perfumes pour in endless cascades in the abounding joy that scatters and gives up and dies every moment.

RABINDRANATH TAGORE

In every life there are certain moments which partake of another, higher order of experience—peculiarly precious moments which offer serenity, hope, and strength and which allow us to return to the de-

mands of daily life with renewed vitality and confidence. The growth
of a spiritual dimension in each of us as individuals seems to result in
a multiplication and a deepening of such moments both in ourselves
and in the world.

ELIZABETH M. JONES

I wanted to live deep and suck out all the marrow of life, . . . to cut a
broad swath . . . , to drive life into a corner, and reduce it to its lowest
terms, and, if it proved to be mean, why then to get the whole and
genuine meanness of it, and publish its meanness to the world; or if
it were sublime, to know it by experience, and be able to give a true
account of it.

HENRY DAVID THOREAU

What truth religions have is not the certitude of reason or logic; but
more like the sureness of the feel of an apple in one's hand.

JACOB TRAPP

It is the reality of human experience that at our core we respond to the universe with a sense of awe and wonder at creation. We are dazzled by the incomprehensible fact of being itself. Through history, we have responded to this sense of awe and wonder with song, with prayers, with dance, with theology, with philosophy, with great art and architecture, with a sense of humility and a recognition that there is something that is both part of us and beyond us, something which we cannot name or control. It is from this sense of awe that the most profound wisdom springs.

MICHAEL LERNER

The religion of the future will be a cosmic religion. It should transcend definitions of God, and avoid dogmas and theology. Covering both the natural and the spiritual, it should be based on a religious sense arising from the experience of all things as meaningful unity.

ALBERT EINSTEIN

Then I was standing on the highest mountain of them all, and round about beneath me was the whole hoop of the world. And while I stood there I saw more than I can tell and I understood more than I saw; for I was seeing in a sacred manner the shapes of all things in the spirit, and the shape of all shapes as they must live together like one being. And I saw that the sacred hoop of my people was one of many hoops that made one circle, wide as daylight and as starlight, and in the center grew one mighty flowering tree to shelter all the children of one mother and one father. And I saw that it was holy.

BLACK ELK

Not greater Marvels around me, not a more divine or a more wonderful world, nor greater opportunity for service—but grant unto me the experiencing mind, the power to realize what is ever here. And when for the moment my awareness fails, grant unto me the continued confidence that those realities which I have seen in great moments are still with me. And so, through experience may I have hope.

FRANK O. HOLMES, INSPIRED BY SAMUEL MCCHORD CROTHERS

We live in all we seek. The hidden shows up in too-plain sight. It lives captive on the face of the obvious—the people, events, and things of the day—to which we as sophisticated children have long since become oblivious. What a hideout: Holiness lies spread and borne over the surface of time and stuff like color.

ANNIE DILLARD

The fairest thing we can experience is the mysterious. It is the fundamental emotion which stands at the cradle of true art and true science. He who knows it not and can no longer wonder, no longer feel amazement, is as good as dead, a snuffed-out candle.

ALBERT EINSTEIN

Nothing any theologian ever wrote about God has helped me very much, but everything that the poets have written about flowers, and birds, and skies, and seas and the saviors of the race, and God—whoever God may be—has at one time or another reached my soul.

JOHN HAYNES HOLMES

He who binds to himself a joy
Does the winged life destroy;
But he who kisses the joy as it flies
Lives in eternity's sun rise.

WILLIAM BLAKE

SECOND SOURCE

Words and deeds of prophetic women and men which challenge us to confront powers and structures of evil with justice, compassion, and the transforming power of love

IN A RELIGION OF DEEDS not creeds, we look to the example of our spiritual ancestors and the prophets of our time for the strength and wisdom to do the right thing. Most religious traditions have their founders, their prophets, and their sages. Unitarian Universalism is no different. We revere people like Francis David, the first clergyperson in the Reformation to proclaim religious tolerance, who said "we need not think alike to love alike." We hold up Theodore Parker, the radical abolitionist minister; Ralph Waldo Emerson, a leader of the Transcendentalist movement; Susan B. Anthony, who fought for women's suffrage; Norbert Fabian Capek, who defied the Nazis; James Reeb, martyred in Selma, Alabama, in the cause for civil rights. And many more.

Yet we do not lift up our own luminaries above all others, saying that only with them will truth be found. We are led to deeper wisdom and action by many outside our own faith story who have spoken to the human condition and the ethical demand to leave the world better than we found it.

Those whom we call prophets include courageous leaders of direct social action—but also those who call for an inner revolution that must precede any transformation in the wider world. Many theologians have reflected on the inseparability of justice, compassion, and love in our engagement with the world. Justice without compassion can lead to legalism and brutality. Loving without a commitment to justice can become mere sentimentality.

The powers and structures of evil surround us. Many religious doctrines try to define and explain them. But we have turned away from theological disputes about evil—focusing instead on faithful encouragement to stand up and confront it.

What do you mean by crushing my people and grinding the faces of the poor?

ISAIAH 3:15

Let your life speak. Have the patience to be silent and listen for truth. Then have the courage to let the best that is in you direct your actions. Recognize that your true identity is nothing more or less than the way in which you conduct your public and private affairs—the way in which, for good or for ill, you let your life speak.

ROBERT LAWRENCE SMITH

If all you can do is light a candle,
tell a story, or keep a promise
Just this day, one more day, every day . . .
Keep us strong in the struggle, bearing witness,
seeking freedom, creating justice
Find a way, build a way, make some way . . .
This we pray, humbly pray, urgently pray.

Clouds of witness surround us,
honored prophets, faithful workers, daring leaders

Speak the truth, heal the world, light the dawn . . .
And we journey together, in the struggle,
make connection, find forgiveness
Through the work, through the pain, moving on . . .
We must build for the future peace and plenty,
truth and justice, hope and freedom
Not oppress, not destroy . . .
Righteousness shines like a golden city, a mighty river,
Bringing hope, bringing peace, bringing forth joy!

In the memory of sacrifice and enduring hope—liberation!
In the dignity and worth of every soul—our salvation!
In the power of love and the human spirit—transformation!
We can change the world. . . .

KENDYL GIBBONS

If you hear the dogs, keep going. If you see the torches in the woods,
keep going. If there's shouting after you, keep going. Don't ever stop,
keep going. If you want a taste of freedom, keep going.

HARRIET TUBMAN, ATTRIBUTED

Over the last few years I have consistently preached that nonviolence demands that the means we use must be as pure as the ends we seek. So I have tried to make it clear that it is wrong to use immoral means to attain moral ends. But now I must affirm that it is just as wrong, or even more so, to use moral means to preserve immoral ends.

MARTIN LUTHER KING JR.

The Divine has no body on earth but yours,
no hands but yours,
no feet but yours,
Yours are the eyes through which the
Divine compassion is to look out to the world.

TERESA OF AVILA

I can count on the fingers of one hand the number of times that I have heard a sermon on the meaning of religion, of Christianity, to the man who stands with his back against the wall. It is urgent that my meaning be crystal clear. The masses of men live with their backs constantly against the wall. They are the poor, the disinherited, the dispossessed. What does our religion say to them? The issue is not what it counsels them to do for others whose need may be greater, but what religion offers to meet their own needs. The search for an answer to this question is perhaps the most important religious quest of modern life.

HOWARD THURMAN

It is a piteous thing to be
Enlisted in no cause at all,
Unsworn to any heraldry;
To fly no banner from the wall, . . .

This were a greater sin against
That hostage in your living breast,
Than to arouse the world incensed
At something you believed your quest, . . .

To take the smooth and middle path,
The half-heart interest, the creed
Without extreme of hope or wrath,
Ah, this were heresy indeed. . . .

SARA HENDERSON HAY

One night I went to the church. They had a mass meeting. And I went to the church, and they talked about how it was our right, that we could register and vote. They were talking about we could vote out people that we didn't want in office, we thought that wasn't right, that we could vote them out. That sounded interesting enough to me that I wanted to try it. I had never heard, until 1962, that black people could register and vote. . . . When they asked for those to raise their hands who'd go down to the courthouse, . . . I raised mine. Had it up high as I could get it. I guess if I'd had any sense I'd've been a little scared, but what was the point of being scared? The only thing they could do to me was kill me and it seemed like they'd been trying to do that a little bit at a time ever since I could remember.

FANNIE LOU HAMER, COMPOSITE

We must not only preach but live by what we had received as truth, or else renounce it honestly as impracticable.

ADIN BALLOU

Be ashamed to die until you have won some victory for humanity.

HORACE MANN

And what does the LORD require of you?
To act justly and to love mercy
and to walk humbly with your God.

MICAH: 6:8

Young people say what good can one person do? What is the sense of our small effort? They cannot see that we must lay one brick at a time, take one step at a time. We can be responsible only for the action of the present moment. But we can beg for an increase of love in our hearts that will vitalize and transform all our individual actions and know that God will take them and multiply them, as Jesus multiplied the loaves and fishes.

DOROTHY DAY

We declare our right on this earth to be a . . . human being, to be respected as a human being, to be given the rights of a human being in this society, on this earth, in this day, which we intend to bring into existence by any means necessary.

MALCOLM X

Conquer anger by love. Conquer evil by good. Conquer the stingy by giving. Conquer the liar by truth.

GAUTAMA BUDDHA

Above the generations the lonely prophets rise,
while truth flares as the daystar within their glowing eyes;
and other eyes, beholding, are kindled from that flame;
and dawn becomes the morning, when prophets love proclaim.

WILLIAM CHANNING GANNETT

If there is among you anyone in need, a member of your community in any of your towns within the land that the LORD your God is giving you, do not be hard-hearted or tight-fisted toward your needy neighbor. You should rather open your hand, willingly lending enough to meet the need, whatever it may be. Be careful that you do not entertain a mean thought, thinking, "The seventh year, the year of remission, is near," and therefore view your needy neighbor with hostility and give nothing; your neighbor might cry to the LORD against you, and you would incur guilt. Give liberally and be ungrudging when you do so, for on this account the LORD your God will bless you in all your work and in all that you undertake. Since there will never cease to be some in need on the earth, I therefore command you, "Open your hand to the poor and needy neighbor in your land."

DEUTERONOMY 15:7–11

Non-violence is like radium in its action. An infinitesimal quantity of it embedded in a malignant growth acts continuously, silently and ceaselessly till it has transformed the whole mass of the diseased tissue into a healthy one. Similarly, even a little of true non-violence acts in a silent, subtle, unseen way and leavens the whole society.

MOHANDAS K. GANDHI

> May those who go in dread have no more fear.
> May captives be unchained and now set free.
> And may the weak receive their strength.
> May living beings help each other in kindness. . . .
>
> And now as long as space endures,
> As long as there are beings to be found,
> May I continue likewise to remain
> To drive away the sorrows of the world.

SHANTIDEVA

Then the men stepped forward, seized Jesus and arrested him. With that, one of Jesus' companions reached for his sword, drew it out and struck the servant of the high priest, cutting off his ear. "Put your sword back in its place," Jesus said to him, "for all who draw the sword will die by the sword."

MATTHEW 26:50–52

When the machetes of injustice
tear apart the fabric of the nation and the world,
I speak up.
When the sunset resembles purple and orange vines
entwined like lovers,
I sigh in silence.
When the mud of deceptions and trickery
smears the mirror of public life,
I speak up.
When the moon rests like a thin slice of lemon
in the sparkling glass of morning,
I smile in silence.
When the insecure bully me,
or the greedy clutch at the common purse,
I speak up.

When a song lifts my soul aloft like a lark,
I swoon in silence.
When wars and rumors of wars destroy
the hopes and lives of children,
I speak up.
When I am overcome by the sheer reality
of a communion of life
connecting every woman, man and child
on this one world earth,
I give thanks in silence.

MARK BELLETINI

Because of those who came before, we are;
in spite of their failings, we believe;
Because of, and in spite of the horizons of their vision,
we, too, dream.

BARBARA PESCAN

Keepers of the dream will come again and again, from what humble places we do not know, to struggle against the crushing odds, leaving behind no worldly kingdom, but only a gleam in the dark hills to show how high we may climb. Already there have been many such heroes—women and men whose names we do not know, but whose words and deeds still light the path for us.

H.G. WENZEL

Many are the windows that will stay darkened unless we light them. It is our watch now! Come great hearts, come dreamers and singers and poets, come builders, come healers, come activists, come those of the soil and those who command the might of machines. Carry the sacred flame to make light the windows of the world. It is we who must be keepers of the flame. It is we who must carry the imperishable fire. It is our watch now! It is our watch now!

TOM OWEN-TOWLE

Those who lived before us,
who struggled for justice
and suffered injustice before us,
have not melted into the dust,
and have not disappeared.
They are with us still.
The lives they lived hold us steady. . . .

We take them with us,
and with them choose
the deeper path of living.

Kathleen McTigue

The measure of what we shall do to men cannot be our wishes about what they shall do to us. For our wishes express not only our right but also our wrong, and our foolishness more than our wisdom. This is the limit of the Golden Rule. This is the limit of calculating justice. Only for him who knows what he should wish and who actually wishes it, is the Golden Rule ultimately valid. Only love can transform calculating justice into creative justice. Love makes justice just. Justice without love is always injustice because it does not do justice to the other one, nor to oneself, nor to the situation in which we meet.

Paul Tillich

As religious liberals, we commit ourselves to principles, purposes, and ideals that are not mere abstractions. They are a conceptualization of the sacred land, a map drawn by those who have, themselves, stood in the presence of glory. With the map comes a promise: If you travel to this country, you will see great beauty.

Rebecca Parker

At times our own light goes out and is rekindled by a spark from another person. Each of us has cause to think with deep gratitude of those who have lighted the flame within us.

ALBERT SCHWEITZER

We are the hearts and minds, the hands and feet, the embodiment of all the best visions of our people.

KATHLEEN McTIGUE

Always it is easier to pay homage to prophets than to heed the direction of their vision.

It is easier blindly to venerate the saints than to learn the human quality of their sainthood.

It is easier to glorify the heroes of the race than to give weight to their examples.

To worship the wise is much easier than to profit by their wisdom.

Great leaders are honored, not by adulation, but by sharing their insights and values. Grandchildren of those who stoned the prophet sometimes gather up the stones to build the prophet's monument.

Always it is easier to pay homage to prophets than to heed the direction of their vision.

Clinton Lee Scott

Let me not cry, "Peace, peace," when there should be no peace in the everlasting war of good against evil, of the better against the worse. Let me not accept as inevitable any unnecessary suffering, or cry "Impossible" before the dream of a more just world. Keep alive within me this day, O Lord, the sacred flame of indignation; help me to say "No" to whatever is inhumane; that by my word and courage the forces of decency and fairness may be strengthened in my time.

Frank Holmes

Is there nothing worth risking the end of one's life for? Are there no dreams or goals so important that we can risk our own destruction to gain them? A Christian willingly chooses to sacrifice himself that other men might be saved. Wherever right is struggling with wrong he takes his place in the battle line. Wherever men are in misery and sickness he gives of himself to relieve their suffering.

James Reeb

Thou that hearest, listen—
In the beginning is the cry—
inarticulate—inchoate—essential. . . .
O, how we must listen
to hear the wanting within the word
O, listen to hear the meaning
in the soul of what is said.

The first act of a prophet
is to hear one's own first cry. . . .

Desire is good
and longing is the first prayer.
Let us bless ourselves with knowing
and bless each other with words that are true.
And let us be glad. Amen.

BARBARA PESCAN

O God, forgive our rich nation where small babies
die of cold quite legally.

O God, forgive our rich nation where small
children suffer from hunger quite legally.

O God, forgive our rich nation where toddlers and
school children die from guns sold quite
legally. . . .

O God, forgive our rich nation that lets the rich
continue to get more at the expense of the
poor quite legally. . . .

O God, help us never to confuse what is quite legal
with what is just and right in Your sight.

MARION WRIGHT EDELMAN

For each child that's born, a morning star rises and sings to
the universe who we are.
We are our grandmothers' prayers and
we are our grandfathers' dreamings,
we are the breath of our ancestors,
we are the spirit of God.
We are mothers of courage and fathers of time,
we are daughters of dust and the sons of great visions,
we're sisters of mercy and brothers of love,
we are lovers of life and the builders of nations,

we're seekers of truth and keepers of faith,
we are makers of peace and the wisdom of ages.

Ysaye M. Barnwell

For all the saints whose perfections and imperfections have shaped my life, I give thanks. Some have traveled with me a long time and witnessed the best and the worst I have offered the world. Others have been with me only briefly. Among these traveling companions are those who have died, but have not vanished. Sometimes they arrive unexpectedly in the middle of my busy days and ask what I'm doing and why. In quiet moments they come to rest in the inner-most part of my soul, telling me I am not alone. Sometimes they arrive as ghosts of my unfinished business. Floating freely through closed doors, they unlock my certainties to remind me of what I did or failed to do for others. My saints don't perform miracles with bags of magic tricks. Rather, they are transformers who change my life.

Stephen Shick

Spirit of Life,
Revealed to us in all who companion our days
And share the work of our hands
We pause to give thanks.
We are grateful for communities of conscience
Which inspire us to step outside of ourselves
And make real those values and beliefs which move us to action.
We give thanks for the truth tellers in our lives,
Prophets and poets whose passion for justice
Stir in us a renewed hope
Of a world made fair, and all her people one,
Turning us now into one more prophet.

KATHLEEN ROLENZ

It is not enough merely to call for freedom, democracy and human rights. There has to be a united determination to persevere in the struggle, to make sacrifices in the name of enduring truths, to resist the corrupting influences of desire, ill will, ignorance, and fear.

AUNG SAN SUU KYI

To see the universal and all-pervading Spirit of Truth face to face one must be able to love the meanest of creation as oneself. And a man who aspires after that cannot afford to keep out of any field of life. That is why my devotion to Truth has drawn me into the field of politics; and I can say without the slightest hesitation, and yet in all humility, that those who say that religion has nothing to do with politics do not know what religion means.

MOHANDAS K. GANDHI

THIRD SOURCE

*Wisdom from the world's religions
which inspires us in our ethical
and spiritual life*

THERE ARE MANY PATHS to truth. Some have been forged through centuries of spiritual practices, sacred texts, communal traditions, and ways of connecting with the Holy. The great religions of the world have discovered ineffable understandings of reality and the human experience.

Unitarian Universalists recognize the wisdom found in cultural traditions throughout history and around the globe. Some UUs go to their congregation to sit in Buddhist meditation, others to study the Bible or to attend a Pagan ritual. Some of us declare dual or multiple religious identities. And some of us—who have well-established connections in Christian, Buddhist, Jewish, and Pagan or Wiccan communities—have found that a Unitarian Universalist congregation offers a spiritual home to us and our families.

Most Unitarian Universalists engage with texts, practices, and rituals from the world's religions as a way to deepen our spiritual lives. We recognize what is common among the many teachings throughout history and draw upon these elements for our worship. All religions may not proclaim a common message, but they do share some universal insights. These are often found in ethical teachings and exhortations towards justice. We learn how to treat one another as we understand our many faiths.

We also find inspiration from the contemplative and devotional practices that have been developed around the world. These time-tested methods of approaching the divine have much to teach us. They can complement and deepen our Unitarian Universalism, not threaten it.

Among the readings gathered here, some reflect what the world's religions have in common; others highlight the special insights that each faith offers uniquely. Like the readings, Unitarian Universalists honor both the general truths of the human experience and the particular gifts of each culture's revelations. We all have more in common than otherwise.

The best form is to worship God in every form.

NEEM KAROLI BABA

If I have any advice for those struggling to discover their own truths, it is found in the ancient wisdom of a Sufi parable: If you want to move beyond a surface understanding of any religious tradition, you've got to dig a well—a well as deep as the self. You have to go into the depths of that tradition if you are to find the living water that awaits your thirst. Stated differently: Find a religious path—any path—and go as deeply as you can to understand and embrace it fully.

MARJORIE BOWENS-WHEATLEY

Each of the great religions has a distinctive note,
to be likened to the strings of a harp.

In Hinduism it is the note of spirit:
a universe throbbing with divine energy and meaning.

In Buddhism it is the wisdom of self discipline:
quenching the fire of desire in the cool waters of meditation.

In Confucianism it is reciprocity:
mutual consideration is the basis of society.

In Taoism it is to conquer by inaction:
be lowly and serviceable, like a brook;
become rich by sharing.

In Judaism it is exodus from bondage:
the covenant of responsibility in freedom.

In Islam it is the note of submission:
"Our God and your God is one, to whom we are self-surrendered."

In Christianity it is that all may become one:
"This is my body broken for you."
"Inasmuch as you have done it to one of the least of these."

JACOB TRAPP

Religion is the first and last—the universal language of the human heart.

Differing words describe the outward appearance of things; diverse symbols represent that which stands beyond and within.

Yet every person's hunger is the same, and heart communicates with heart.

Ever the vision leads on with many gods or with one, with a holy land washed by ocean waters, or a holy land within the heart.

W. WALDEMAR W. ARGOW

Unto the church universal, which is the depository of all ancient wisdom and the school of all modern thought;

Which recognizes in all prophets a harmony, in all scriptures a unity, and through all dispensations a continuity;

Which abjures all that separates and divides, and always magnifies all that unifies and brings peace;

Which seeks truth in freedom, justice in love, and individual discipline in social duty;

And which shall make of all sects, classes, nations, and races, one global community;

Unto this church and unto all its members, known and unknown throughout the world,

We pledge the allegiance of our hands and hearts.

KESHAB CHANDRA SEN, ARRANGED BY JOHN HAYNES HOLMES

A dialogue by members of the world community which promotes peace requires risk. The risk includes the possibility of arousing anger and hostility in the expression of strongly held conflicting views. Perhaps an even greater risk is the surprise in receiving new insights that require changing your own perspective. It is possible that you could discover unexplored horizons of meaning and truth. In real engagement with another person, you cannot fully foresee what will happen. At the same time, risk must be matched by trust. To expose yourself to the analysis and challenge of another person requires trust. Dialogue depends on trust that the other person is also caring, is secure enough in his or her view to allow for differences, and is open to learning new dimensions of his or her orientation that may be evoked in dialogue.

FREDERICK J. STRENG

When you and I look at these trees, these flowers, anything at all, we are the universe looking at its handiwork. You have perhaps seen the pattern of cross and yarn called the "eye of God" made first in our Southwest in homage to the sun. We, too, all of us together, all the eyes of all the creatures, are the eye of God. That is why we need each other, our many ways of seeing, that together we may rejoice, and see clearly, and find the many keys to abundant life.

GRETA W. CROSBY

To clasp the hands in prayer is the beginning of an uprising against the disorder of the world.

KARL BARTH

I think that one of our most important tasks is to convince others that there's nothing to fear in difference; that difference, in fact, is one of the healthiest and most invigorating of human characteristics without which life would become meaningless. Here lies the power of the liberal way: not in making the whole world Unitarian, but in helping ourselves and others to see some of the possibilities inherent in viewpoints other than one's own; in encouraging the free interchange of ideas; in welcoming fresh approaches to the problems of life; in urging the fullest, most vigorous use of critical self-examination.

ADLAI STEVENSON

The light of this chalice reminds us
that it is a symbol
of all the world's religions.
This small light shines
as do the fires burned
to ward off the darkness
and welcome back the sun
in the Celtic and Native American faiths;
as do the Jewish Shabbat candles
and the Christian altar candles;
as do the oil lamps of the Hindu Divali
and the candles of Buddhism;
and it is a symbol of the light inside each of us, as recognized
        by Muslims;
it is a symbol of the sun
and evolution as studied by Humanists.
As we light this chalice,
may we be reminded that this light
is a symbol that ties us to many faiths,

beliefs, traditions, and customs
from which we can learn and enrich our lives.

BETH CASEBOLT

Because she wanted everyone to feel included
in her prayer,
she said right at the beginning
several names for the Holy:
Spirit, she said. *Holy One, Mystery, God*

but then thinking these weren't enough ways of addressing
that which cannot be fully addressed, she added
particularities, saying *Spirit of Life, Spirit of Love,*
Ancient Holy One, Mystery We Will Not Ever Fully Know,
Gracious God and also *Spirit of this Earth,*
God of Sarah, Gaia, Thou

and then, tongue loosened, she fell to naming
superlatives as well: *Most Creative One,*
Greatest Source, Closest Hope—
even though superlatives for the Sacred seemed to her
probably redundant, but then she couldn't stop:

One Who Made the Stars, she said, although she knew
technically a number of those present didn't believe
the stars had been made by anyone or thing
but just luckily happened.
One who Is an Entire Ocean of Compassion,
she said, and no one laughed.

That Which Has Been Present Since Before the Beginning,
she said, and the room was silent.

Then, although she hadn't imagined it this way,
Others began to offer names:

Peace, said one.
One My Mother Knew, said another.
Ancestor, said a third.
Wind.
Rain.
Breath, said one near the back.
Refuge.
That Which Holds All.
A child said, *Water.*
Someone said, *Kuan Yin.*
Then: *Womb.*
Witness.

Great Kindness.
Eternal Stillness.

And then, there wasn't any need to say the things
she'd thought would be important to say,
and everyone sat hushed, until someone said

Amen.

NANCY SHAFFER

Many windows, one light;
Many waters, one sea;
All lifted hearts are free.

In the Talmud of the Jewish tradition, the sage Hillel said: What is
hateful to you, do not do to others. This is the whole of the Law; all
the rest is commentary.

In the Hindu legend of the Mahabharata, the divine Krishna declared:
This is the sum of duty: Do nothing unto others which would cause
you pain if done to you.

In the Gospel of Matthew in the Christian scriptures, the messiah Jesus says: Whatever you wish that others would do to you, do so to them.

In the Buddhist text of the Udanavarga, the student is urged: Hurt not others in ways that you yourself would find hurtful.

In the Muslim Hadith of al Nawawi, the prophet Mohammed teaches: No one of you is a believer until he desires for his brother that which he desires for himself.

In the T'ai Shang treatise of Taoism, the seeker is instructed: Regard your neighbor's gain as your gain, and your neighbor's loss as your own loss.

In the ancient wisdom of Shinto there is a saying: The heart of the person before you is a mirror. See there your own form.

The Oglala Lakota spiritual leader Black Elk wrote: All things are our relatives; what we do to everything, we do to ourselves.

It is written; it is taught; may it be so.

Many windows, one light;
Many waters, one sea;
All lifted hearts are free.

Shanti, shalom; hasiti, salaam; heiwa, dohiyi; pax, paco, mir . . .
Peace . . .

KENDYL GIBBONS

Just then a lawyer stood up to test Jesus. "Teacher," he said, "what must I do to inherit eternal life?"

He said to him, "What is written in the law? What do you read there?"

He answered, "You shall love the Lord your God with all your heart, and with all your soul, and with all your strength, and with all your mind; and your neighbor as yourself."

And he said to him, "You have given the right answer; do this, and you will live."

But wanting to justify himself, he asked Jesus, "And who is my neighbor?"

Jesus replied, "A man was going down from Jerusalem to Jericho, and fell into the hands of robbers, who stripped him, beat him, and went away, leaving him half dead.

Now by chance a priest was going down that road; and when he saw him, he passed by on the other side.

So likewise a Levite, when he came to the place and saw him, passed by on the other side.

But a Samaritan while traveling came near him; and when he saw him, he was moved with pity.

He went to him and bandaged his wounds, having poured oil and wine on them. Then he put him on his own animal, brought him to an inn, and took care of him.

The next day he took out two denarii, gave them to the innkeeper, and said, 'Take care of him; and when I come back, I will repay you whatever more you spend.'

Which of these three, do you think, was a neighbor to the man who fell into the hands of the robbers?"

He said, "The one who showed him mercy." Jesus said to him, "Go and do likewise."

LUKE 10:25–37

Today children are born into a swirl of cultures, races, and religions. Whether we encourage or limit independence of thought, our children take for granted the bustling marketplace of ideas where so many religious orientations compete for legitimacy. I've come to realize just how many people are choosing to construct a sustaining philosophy of life from many different beliefs and values.

LINDA R. WELTNER

We have not chosen God; He has chosen us. There is no concept of a chosen God but there is the idea of a chosen people. The idea of a chosen people does not suggest the preference for a people based upon a discrimination among a number of peoples. We do not say that we are a superior people. The "chosen people" means a people approached and chosen by God. The significance of this term is genuine in relation to God rather than in relation to other peoples. It signifies not a quality inherent in the people but a relationship between the people and God.

ABRAHAM JOSHUA HESCHEL

Rabbi Yochanan ben Zakkai said to them:
What is a right path?
Rabbi Eliezer said: A good eye.
Rabbi Joshua said: A good friend.
Rabbi Yosé said: A good neighbor.
Rabbi Simeon said: Foresight.
Rabbi Elazar said: A good heart.
He said to them:
I prefer the words of Elazar ben Arach,
for his words include all of yours.

MISHNAH

Know this, and you will be free:
Where do you come from?
Where are you going?
To whom do you give an account?

MISHNAH

Bring me a fruit from that tree.
Here it is, venerable Sir.
Cut it open.
It is cut open, venerable Sir.
What do you see in it?
Very small seeds, venerable Sir.
Cut open one of them.
It is cut open, venerable Sir.
What do you see in it?
Nothing, venerable Sir.
Then he said:
That hidden thing which you cannot see,
O gentle youth,
from that hidden thing
has this mighty tree grown.

UPANISHAD

Meditation, like a cool lake, has room for all the unexpected birds.

JACOB TRAPP

One day, the Buddha appeared at an assembly of thousands who were all waiting for him to speak, but the Buddha didn't say a word. He just held up a flower, twirled it, and blinked his eyes. His disciples were greatly confused and each did their best to expound on the meaning of the flower. One offered a lecture; another composed a poem and still a third told a parable. His disciple Mahakashyapa was silent and then began to laugh. Buddha handed the lotus to Mahakasyapa and spoke to the assembly: "What can be said I have said to you," smiled the Buddha, "and what cannot be said, I have given to Mahakashyapa."

BUDDHIST PARABLE

Beings are numberless; I vow to save them.
Delusions are inexhaustible; I vow to end them.
Dharma gates are boundless; I vow to enter them.
The Buddha way is unsurpassable; I vow to embody it.

THE FOUR BODHISATTVA VOWS

And what, monks, is the middle path, by which
the one who has thus come has gained enlightenment,
which produces knowledge and insight,
and leads to peace, wisdom, enlightenment, and nirvana?

This is the noble eightfold way, namely,
correct understanding, correct intention,
correct speech, correct action, correct livelihood,
correct attention, correct concentration,
and correct meditation.

GAUTAMA BUDDHA

To refrain from evil,
To achieve the good,
To purify one's own mind
This is the teaching of all Awakened Ones.

GAUTAMA BUDDHA

To study the Way is to study the self. To study the self is to forget the self. To forget the self is to be enlightened by all things. To be enlightened by all things is to remove the barriers between one's self and others.

Dogen

Ten thousand flowers in spring, the moon in autumn,
a cool breeze in summer, snow in winter.
If your mind isn't clouded by unnecessary things,
this is the best season of your life.

Wu-men

My daily affairs are quite ordinary;
but I'm in total harmony with them.
I don't hold on to anything, don't reject anything;
nowhere an obstacle or conflict.
Who cares about wealth and honor?
Even the poorest thing shines.
My miraculous power and spiritual activity:
Drawing water and carrying wood.

Layman P'ang

The Buddha once told this story about faith: A herd of cows arrives at the bank of a wide stream. The mature ones see the stream and simply wade across it. The Buddha likened them to fully enlightened beings who have crossed the stream of ignorance and suffering. The younger cows, less mature in their wisdom, stumble apprehensively on the shore, but eventually they go forward and cross the stream. Last come the calves, trembling with fear, some just learning how to stand. But these vulnerable, tender calves also get to the other side, the Buddha said. They cross the stream just by following the lowing of their mothers. The calves trust their mothers and, anticipating the safety of reunion, follow their voices and cross the stream. That, the Buddha said, is the power of faith to call us forward.

SHARON SALZBERG

My religion is very simple, my religion is kindness.

THE DALAI LAMA

In all ten directions of the universe,
there is only one truth.
When we see clearly, the great teachings are the same.
What can ever be lost? What can be attained?

If we attain something, it was there from the beginning of time.
If we lose something, it is hiding somewhere near us.
Look: this ball in my pocket:
can you see how priceless it is?

RYŌKAN

God brings forth the living from the dead,
and brings forth the dead from the living;
and God enlivens the earth after its death:
and so will you all be brought forth.

QUR'AN 30:19

We created you from a single (pair) of a male and a female, and made
you into nations and tribes, that ye may know each other (not that ye
may despise each other). Verily the most honored of you in the sight
of God is (he who is) the most righteous of you. And God has full
knowledge and is well acquainted (with all things).

QUR'AN 49:13

In the name of Allah, Most Gracious, Most Merciful.
Praise be to Allah, the Cherisher and Sustainer of the Worlds;
Most Gracious. Most Merciful;
Master of the Day of Judgment.
You do we worship, and Your aid do we seek.
Show us the straight way.
The way of those on whom You have bestowed Your Grace,
those whose (portion) is not wrath, and who do not go astray.

QUR'AN 1:1–7

Repel (Evil) with what is better: Then will he between whom and
thee was hatred become as it were thy friend and intimate!

And no one will be granted such goodness except those who
exercise patience and self-restraint.

QUR'AN 41:34–35

Acquire knowledge. . . . Knowledge enables its possessor to distin-
guish what is forbidden from what is not; it lights the way to Heaven;
it is our friend in the desert, our companion in solitude, our companion when bereft of friends; it guides us to happiness; it sustains us in

misery; it is our ornament in the company of friends; it serves as an
armor against our enemies.

Muhammad

No man is true in the truest sense of the word but he who is true in
word, in deed, and in thought.
Strive always to excel in virtue and truth.
It is not worthy of a speaker of truth to curse people.
Appropriate to yourselves the truth. Avoid lying.
Say what is true, although it may be bitter and displeasing to people.

Muhammad

True servants of God
are those who walk humbly
on the earth and say: "Peace!"
to the ignorant who accost them.

Qur'an 25:63

Do they not observe the birds above them
spreading their wings and folding them?
None could hold them except
the Compassionate Allah;
surely it is He Who watches
over all things.

QUR'AN 67:19

From the Son of Heaven down to the mass of the people, all must
consider the cultivation of the person the root of everything besides.

CONFUCIUS

Oh Almighty! Lead us from the unreal (falsity)
to the real (truth) from darkness to light!
From death to immortality!
Oh Almighty! May there be Peace! Peace! Peace!

BRIHADARANYAKA UPANISADA 1:3:28

Whatever name may have been given to the divine Reality it has found its highest place in the history of our religion owing to its human character, giving meaning to the idea of sin and sanctity, and offering an eternal background to all the ideals of perfection which have their harmony with man's own nature.

RABINDRANATH TAGORE

The ancients who followed Tao:
Dark, wondrous, profound, penetrating,
Deep beyond knowing.

Because they cannot be known,
They can only be described.

Cautious,
Like crossing a winter stream.
Hesitant,
Like respecting one's neighbors.
Polite,
    Like a guest.
Yielding,
    Like ice about to melt.
Blank,
    Like uncarved wood.

Open,
> Like a valley.
Mixing freely,
> Like muddy water.
Calm the muddy water,
> It becomes clear.
Move the inert,
> It comes to life.
Those who sustain Tao
> Do not wish to be full.
Because they do not wish to be full
> They can fade away
>> Without further effort.

LAO TZU

Not Christian or Jew or Muslim, not Hindu,
Buddhist, sufi or zen. Not any religion

or cultural system. I am not from the East
or the West, not out of the ocean or up

from the ground, not natural or ethereal, not
composed of elements at all. I do not exist,

am not an entity in this world or the next,
did not descend from Adam and Eve or any

origin story. My place is placeless, a trace
of the traceless. Neither body or soul.

I belong to the beloved, have seen the two
worlds as one and that one call to and know,

first, last, outer, inner, only that
breath breathing human being.

RUMI

Blessing of fish and birds, blessing of mammals:
    Salmon, eagle, cougar and mountain goat.

May all humankind likewise offer blessing. . . .

Bless the wisdom of the holy one above us;
Bless the truth of the holy one beneath us;
Bless the love of the holy one within us.

CHINOOK PSALTER

"We cast our prayers seven generations ahead." Many Native people say this. Also we say that we listen to the ancestors, so we cast our prayers seven generations behind, too, as we try to hear the memories that come before the individual memories we believe are our own. We are, of course, someone's seventh generation. Back in the spiral of time, someone prayed for us and hoped we would listen and hear. Our stories create our world.

JANICE GOULD

FOURTH SOURCE

Jewish and Christian teachings

which call us to respond to

God's love by loving

our neighbors

as ourselves

OUR CONGREGATION sat in silence and in near darkness as each candle in the Tenebrae service was extinguished. We felt the loss palpably as the story of Jesus' betrayal and crucifixion was told. When the voice singing "Were you there when they crucified my Lord," rose to the ceiling of the chapel, our tears surprised and overwhelmed us. This service is held on Maundy Thursday each year, attracting Christians and non-Christians alike. Members of both the congregation and the larger community come, drawn to a Unitarian Universalist setting to commemorate the life of one of the world's greatest prophets and teachers.

The following evening, we gather again, to participate in the annual Seder dinner, open to all, but especially to families who have a Jewish heritage. The reading of the Seder Haggadah is always led by a member who speaks Hebrew, and who can remind the gathered of the sacrifices made by the Israelites many years ago for their freedom. The Seder ritual meal elements are laid out carefully—matzoh, wine, a boiled egg, haroset, bitter herbs, a lamb shank. Candles are lit and we feel a sense of great reverence as we go back in time to the very first Passover—Unitarian Universalist, Jew, and non-Jew sitting side by side. After the dinner, children look for the afikoman.

These two great religions—Christianity and Judaism—are two interwoven strands that compose the fabric of our faith. Both Unitarianism and Universalism were Protestant traditions that understood themselves to be following the teachings of Jesus in a form unadulterated by centuries of Christian Church tradition. Also, Jesus was a Jew and the religion he taught arose out of Jewish stories, values, and teachings before his followers developed it into a religion about him. Many Unitarian Universalists recognize the inadequacies of lumping Judaism and Christianity into something called "the Judeo-Christian" tradition. We honor the special place that both traditions hold in our history and in the current practice of many of our members.

Even Unitarian Universalists who aren't very familiar with Judaism often find inspiration in the sacred Jewish texts, discovering fresh meaning and insight in them when explored within the context of a Unitarian Universalist community. In addition to sharing a Seder meal together, many Unitarian Universalists incorporate Yom Kippur and Hanukkah observations into their worship life. Hebrew scriptures are read and studied and often are woven into the fabric of the liturgical year.

Likewise, the teachings of Jesus and the letters of Paul invite Unitarian Universalists into the insights available from a deeper relationship with liberal Christianity. Allowing the accretions of dogma that often surround the teachings of Jesus to dissolve, we see with fresh eyes the essence of his message. We can resonate with the second half of his Great Commandment, cited from the Torah, "Thou shalt love thy neighbor as thyself." Through the spirit of Jesus' message we can claim him as teacher, prophet, and guide—and freely examine and call upon this Source as one of the deep wells from which we draw.

Hear, O Israel: The LORD our God, the LORD is one. Love the LORD your God with all your heart and with all your soul and with all your strength. These commandments that I give you today are to be upon your hearts.

DEUTERONOMY 6: 4–6

If I am not for myself, who will be for me?
And if I am for myself alone, what am I?
And if not now, when?

HILLEL THE ELDER

God is not hiding in a temple. The Torah came to tell inattentive man: "You are not alone, you live constantly in holy neighborhood; remember: 'Love thy neighbor—God—as thyself.'" We are . . . asked . . . to keep the spark within aflame, and to suffer His light to reflect in our face.

ABRAHAM JOSHUA HESCHEL

I call heaven and earth to witness . . . that I have set before you life and death, the blessing and the curse: therefore choose life, that you may live, you and your seed.

DEUTERONOMY 30:19

Some Hasidim of the Maggid of Mezheritz came to him. "Rebbe, we are puzzled. It says in the Talmud that we must thank God as much for the bad days, as for the good. How can that be? What would our gratitude mean, if we gave it equally for the good and the bad?"

The Maggid replied, "Go to Anapol. Reb Zusya will have an answer for you."

The Hasidim undertook the journey. Arriving in Anapol, they inquired for Reb Zusya. At last, they came to the poorest street of the city. There, crowded between two small houses, they found a tiny shack, sagging with age.

When they entered, they saw Reb Zusya sitting at a bare table, reading a volume by the light of the only small window. "Welcome, strangers!" he said. "Please pardon me for not getting up; I have hurt my leg. Would you like food? I have some bread. And there is water!"

"No. We have come only to ask you a question. The Maggid of Mezheritz told us you might help us understand: Why do our sages tell us to thank God as much for the bad days as for the good?"

Reb Zusya laughed. "Me? I have no idea why the Maggid sent

you to me." He shook his head in puzzlement. "You see, I have never had a bad day. Every day God has given to me has been filled with miracles."

HASIDIC STORY

A king was told that a man of humility is endowed with long life. He attired himself in old garments, took up his residence in a small hut, and forbade anyone to show reverence before him. But when he honestly examined himself, the king found himself to be prouder of his seeming humility than ever before. A philosopher thereupon remarked to him: "Dress like a king; live like a king; allow the people to show due respect to you; but be humble in your inmost heart. "

BAAL SHEM TOV

Sim shalom tovah uvrachah chen vachesed v'rachamim aleinu v'al kol Yisrael amecha.

Grant us peace, Your most precious gift, O Eternal Source of peace, and give us the will to proclaim its message to all the peoples of the earth. Bless our country, that it may always be a stronghold of peace, and its advocate among the nations. May contentment reign within its borders, health and happiness within its homes. Strengthen the bonds of friendship among the inhabitants of all lands, and may the love of Your name hallow every home and every heart. Blessed is the Eternal God, the Source of peace.

JEWISH PRAYER

We pray that we might know before whom we stand:
the Power whose gift is life,
who quickens those who have forgotten how to live.
We pray for the winds to disperse the choking air of sadness,
for cleansing rains to make parched hopes flower,
and to give all of us the strength to rise up toward the sun.

We pray for love to encompass us
for no other reason save that we are human,
for love through which we may all blossom into persons
who have gained power over our own lives.

We pray to stand upright, we fallen;
to be healed, we sufferers;
we pray to break the bonds that keep us from the world of
beauty;
we pray for opened eyes,
we who are blind to our own authentic selves.

We pray that we may walk in the garden of a purposeful life,
our own powers in touch with the power of the world.

Praised be the God whose gift is life,
whose cleansing rains let parched men and women
flower toward the sun.

JEWISH PRAYER

The miracle of Exodus is that a group of people finally realized for
themselves, for us, and for all time that you cannot stay in Egypt.
Any personal commitment that is not toward growing and changing,
any religious commitment that is not toward goals beyond one's own
personal welfare, is a commitment toward slavery in Egypt.

JOHN NICHOLS

One of the teachers of the law came and heard them debating. No-
ticing that Jesus had given them a good answer, he asked him, "Of
all the commandments, which is the most important?" "The most
important one," answered Jesus, "is this: 'Hear, O Israel, the Lord
our God, the Lord is one. Love the Lord your God with all your
heart and with all your soul and with all your mind and with all your

strength.' The second is this: 'Love your neighbor as yourself.' There is no commandment greater than these."

MARK 12:28–31

O, Birther! Father-Mother of the Cosmos,

Focus your light within us — make it useful:

Create your reign of unity now—

Your one desire then acts with ours,
as in all light, so in all forms.

Grant what we need each day in bread and insight.

Loose the cords of mistakes binding us,
as we release the strands we hold
of others' guilt.

Don't let surface things delude us,

But free us from what holds us back.

From you is born all ruling will,
the power and the life to do,
the song that beautifies all,
from age to age it renews.

Truly—power to these statements—
may they be the ground from which all
my actions grow: Amen.

ARAMAIC PRAYER OF JESUS

Once Jesus was asked by the Pharisees when the kingdom of God was coming, and he answered, "The kingdom of God is not coming with things that can be observed; nor will they say, 'Look, here it is!' or 'There it is!' For, in fact, the kingdom of God is among you."

LUKE 17:20–21

I want to thank You, Lord
For life and all that's in it.
Thank You for the day
And for the hour and for the minute.
I know many are gone,

I'm still living on,
I want to thank You.

MAYA ANGELOU

O Holy Spirit, love of God, infuse thy grace,
And descend plentifully into my heart;
Enlighten the dark corners of this neglected dwelling,
And scatter there thy cheerful beams;
Dwell in that soul that longs to be thy temple;
Water that barren soil, overrun with weeds and briars,
And lost for want of cultivating,
And make it fruitful with thy dew from heaven.

AUGUSTINE OF HIPPO

O God, whose love is over all
The children of thy grace.
Whose rich and tender blessings fall
On every age and place,
Hear thou the songs and prayers we raise
In eager joy to thee,

And teach us, as we sound thy praise,
In all things thee to see.

JOHN HAYNES HOLMES

My central story of freedom is the liberating biblical story of Jesus, another touchstone for me. God is present there, but he is also present in other great stories of freedom found in science, philosophy, art, and humanities; in other religions; and in people's contemporary lives. Unitarian Universalism brings me into contact with all of the myriad ways God speaks to us today.

Finally, to really follow in the spirit of Jesus means to be in right relationship with those who are different from me, to find mutual healing and transformation in such relationships. In Unitarian Universalism I have many rich opportunities for such encounters.

RON ROBINSON

God is in the nitty gritty work of loving one another in the social, economic, political, and material world. We are called to understand the world's systems and its evils and to establish mutual love in spite of all our unlovability. At the same time, through attention to prayer we discover God, who beckons us to know Mystery in life, we dis-

cover a Love without beginning or end in which we live, which lives
in us, and which offers us unimaginable joy beyond our expectations.

ELIZABETH ELLIS

Speak to Him thou for He hears, and
Spirit with Spirit can meet—
Closer is He than breathing, and nearer
than hands and feet.

ALFRED LORD TENNYSON

God of life and love and mystery.
God of one thousand names.

Too much am I Ishmael, crying in the desert.
Where is your face, if you have so many names?
Too much am I Sarah, casting off bad decisions—banishing
Inconvenience out to the desert to die.
Where is the blessing, if yours is the kingdom at hand?
Too much am I Abraham, indecisive, passive in the face of conflict.
Where is the covenant, if the covenant is for love's sake alone?

Too much am I in exile, too much in Babylon,
Too much weeping in this foreign land,
And I, far from home, can't sing my holy songs.

So where is the prophet, the teacher, if finally comes the poet singing:
"Comfort, O, comfort my people"?

We wait and we wait.

Shake me up in my complacency;
I feel like going on.
Shake me up in my delirium;
I will not be moved.
Quicken in me this sense of love;
I too have a dream.

ROGER BUTTS

God of our weary years, God of our silent tears,
Thou who has brought us thus far on the way;
Thou who hast by thy might, led us into the light,
Keep us forever in the path, we pray.
Lest our feet stray from the places
Our God where we met Thee,
Lest our hearts drunk with the wine of the world

we forget Thee;
Shadowed beneath Thy hand
May we forever stand,
True to our God,
True to our native land.

J<small>AMES</small> W<small>ELDON</small> J<small>OHNSON</small>

Infinite Spirit who needs no words for us to converse with You, we would enter into Your presence. We revere your power; we worship Your wisdom; we are gladdened by Your love and blessed by our communion with You. We live in Your world; we taste Your bounty; we breathe Your air. Your power sustains us; Your justice guides us; Your goodness preserves us; Your love blesses us forever and ever.

T<small>HEODORE</small> P<small>ARKER</small>

Love your enemies, do good to those who hate you, bless those who curse you, pray for those who abuse you. . . . From anyone who takes away your coat do not withhold even your shirt. Give to everyone who begs from you; and if anyone takes away your goods, do not ask for them again.

L<small>UKE</small> 6:27–30

How can we come to You, O God, with hearts that we have closed to one another?

O Holy One, remind us! We are Your children, all, lighted by the same precarious flame. How foolish are our walls of prejudice, our empty pride!

O patient God, take pity on us! You who breathed into us the one breath of our common life, breathe yet again, and bring us to our souls' awakening.

A. POWELL DAVIES

GOD, I'm not trying to rule the roost,
    I don't want to be king of the mountain.
I haven't meddled where I have no business
    or fantasized grandiose plans.

I've kept my feet on the ground,
    I've cultivated a quiet heart.
Like a baby content in its mother's arms,
    my soul is a baby content.

PSALM 131

Palm Sunday is found:

> whenever we are serving a noble and unpopular cause with selfless devotion, holding to the ideals of truth and justice;

> whenever we are seeking to uplift the fallen, to comfort the brokenhearted, to strengthen and encourage the weak and hopeless;

> whenever we are working bravely and persistently in the face of abuse and criticism to establish more equitable relations in the world;

> whenever we are sacrificing our lives in behalf of what we believe to be the service of love for all humanity.

That is Palm Sunday!

DAVID RANKIN

Do to others as you would have them do to you.

LUKE 6:31

I find Jesus of Nazareth a compelling teacher, master poet, trouble-maker, and insistent companion on the 'narrow path,' which is to say reality. Jesus is a spiritual genius, one of many we may choose to learn from, but still the one who most compels me to become the person I am meant to be.

STEPHEN KENDRICK

"This is my commandment, that you love one another as I have loved you. No one has greater love than this, to lay down one's life for one's friends."

JOHN 15:12–13

"Thou shalt love the Lord thy God with thy whole heart, with thy whole soul, and with all thy mind." (Mt. 22:37) This is the command of the great God, and he cannot command the impossible. Love is a fruit in season at all times and within reach of every hand. Anyone may gather it and no limit is set. Everyone can reach this love through meditation—spirit of prayer—and sacrifices, by an intense interior life. Do I really live this life?

MOTHER TERESA

I hold myself bound . . . never . . . to kill, assault, beat, torture, enslave, rob, oppress, persecute, defraud, corrupt, slander, revile, injure, envy, or hate any human being, even my worst enemy.

HOPEDALE COMMUNITY ENTRANCE DECLARATION

The end of Christianity seems to be to make all [people] one with God as Christ was one with [God]; to bring them to such a state of obedience and goodness that we shall think divine thoughts and feel divine sentiments, and so keep the law of God by living a life of truth and love. Its means are purity and prayer; getting strength from God, and using it for our [sisters and brothers] as well as ourselves. It allows perfect freedom. It does not demand all [people] to think alike, but to think uprightly, and get as near as possible at truth; not all [people] to live alike, but to live holy, and get as near as possible to a life perfectly divine.

THEODORE PARKER

Over and over again my Unitarian Universalism has proved not an impediment to my Christian faith but a powerful aid. To be sure, the kind of Christian path I follow is not what many people mean by *Christianity*, but then I've never said I was a Pentecostal Christian or an Evangelical Christian—I am a Unitarian Universalist Christian. By this I mean that I am one who sees in the stories of Jesus the memories of a man whose union with the sacred was complete. He invited people into the mystery he called "God." I see in him the clearest example of the kind of life I wish to live, but I have no problem understanding that other people find clearer examples elsewhere. I find in the person of Jesus a present-day companion on my spiritual journey—challenging me, encouraging me, and supporting me as I pursue a pathless quest into the heart of the mystery itself.

ERIK WALKER WIKSTROM

I don't preach a social gospel; I preach the Gospel, period. The gospel of our Lord Jesus Christ is concerned for the whole person. When people were hungry, Jesus didn't say, "Now is that political or social?" He said, "I feed you." Because the good news to a hungry person is bread.

DESMOND TUTU

Although I wouldn't quite call myself a "follower" of Jesus, I wish to live in the spirit of the historical Jesus and also the Jesus I believe lives today, in the way that we all live after our bodily demise. . . . Although I do not always know how to apply general principles to particular situations, my ideal is pacifism, and I wish to extend that principle to our relations with nonhuman animals that share the life of the world with us. I believe that the birds, beasts, fishes, and quite possibly other life forms will be included in the final harmony of all souls with God.

JOHN SIMCOX

The promised land is not a destination—it is a way of going. The land beyond the Jordan, that country of freedom and dignity and laughter—you carry it inside you all the while. It is planted in your mind and heart already, before you ever start out, before it even occurs to you that in order to leave that life in Egypt, the intolerable bondage of that life, what you need to do is stand up and walk forward.

VICTORIA SAFFORD

FIFTH SOURCE

Humanist teachings which counsel us to heed the guidance of reason and the results of science, and warn us against idolatries of the mind and spirit

"Weave me no fairytales frosted with miracles; Give me a light I can see; Spin me no promise of heavens and saviors, teach me the truth that makes us free." The verse of minister Kendyl Gibbons flows from her deep well of humanist conviction—a faith in the spirituality of the natural, rather than super-natural world, and of ethical principles. Many of us, along with Gibbons, hold that religion at its best is an expression of human values.

We take joy with others in the life of the mind and the tests of reason applied to philosophical and theological claims. We celebrate our ever-expanding knowledge of the mysteries of life through the sciences and the arts. Our moments of awe and praise may come from peering through a microscope and seeing the infinity of the world beneath the glass, or by studying the vast complexities of human nature. We engage with the realities of evolution with an open and eager mind—but also a heart filled with appreciation for the constantly evolving world and our place in it. Humanism encourages the free expression of the human mind and the full expression of the human heart.

We live in an age of religious fundamentalism that threatens not only democratic societies but the peace and stability of the world community. But the humanist view of religious living and its critique of exclusive and "infallible" religious claims offer a saving message.

I would live simply, and bravely and nobly;
Let no illusions remain;
I would seek wisdom in human reality,
Even if wisdom be pain.

Sing me no pious amens and old canticles,
Let doubts and questions arise;
Tell me no providence hidden in prophecies,
But welcome the future's surprise. . . .

Weave me no fairytales frosted with miracles;
Give me a light I can see;
Spin me no promise of heavens and saviors,
Teach me the truth that makes us free.

Create my salvation in earth's endless wonder;
Everything nature provides;
Let me be honest, and wise in compassion;
Make reason and conscience my guides.

Beautiful universe, fathomless energy,
Mysteries we struggle to know;
This is our paradise; dust is our destiny;
Cherish the years as they go.

The time is now, the place is here;
The good we know, the earth we share;
This day we have, this love we give;
No other truth; no other joy;
No other life; no other world.

KENDYL GIBBONS

The human race is a vast rainbow, white, black, red, yellow and brown
bursting into view.
Yet for all,
blood is red,
the sky is blue,
the earth brown,
the night dark.

In size and shape we are a varied pattern of
tall and short,
slim and stout,
elegant and plain.
Yet for all there are
fingers to touch,
hearts to break,
eyes to cry,
ears to hear, mouths to speak.

In tongue we are a tower of babel,
a great jumble of voices grasping for words,
groping for ways to say love, peace, pity, and hope.

Faiths compete, claiming the one way;
saviors abound, pointing to salvation.
Not all can be right, not one.
We are united only by our urge to search.

Boundaries divide us, lines drawn to mark our diversity,
maps charted to separate the human race from itself.
Yet a mother's grief,
a father's love,
a child's happy cry,
a musician's sound,
an artist's stroke,
batter the boundaries and shatter the walls.

Strength and weakness,
arrogance and humility,
confidence and fear,
live together in each one,
reminding us that we share a our common humanity.
We are all more human than otherwise.

RICHARD GILBERT

Stop talking and listen to what you really know. Not everything you comprehend comes from books or from teachers. You know a lot of big and important things in your heart and through your common sense. Learning to trust your own mind, with its wonderful richness and versatility, is how you find out who you really are, what makes you tick. Hold high expectations for yourself and for others. People rise to expectations. Listen to your gut; trust your instincts and your common sense. We are versatile creatures, and we can adjust to change, improvise, and proceed "as way opens."

ROBERT LAWRENCE SMITH

Instead of wanting to curl my mind up and tuck it away in some cozy little place where it could never think those terrifying thoughts of death and birth and time, my mind suddenly wanted to reach out and embrace fearlessly those mysteries and become a conscious, proud part of them.

KATHERINE BUTLER HATHAWAY

This is the mission of our faith:
To teach the fragile art of hospitality;
To revere both the critical mind and the generous heart;

To prove that diversity need not mean divisiveness;
And to witness to all that we must hold the whole world in our hands.

WILLIAM F. SCHULZ

You have to go beyond words and conceptualized ideas and just get into what you are, deeper and deeper. The first glimpse is not quite enough; you have to examine the details without judging, without using words and concepts. Opening to oneself fully is opening to the world.

CHÖGYAM TRUNGPA

We come to our religious values experientially. The beliefs we hold are not so much revealed to us as experienced by us. We encourage our children to develop their own working wisdoms instead of their inheriting the truths of their parents or tradition. All who would participate in our Unitarian Universalist cradle-to-grave religious adventure have the opportunity to develop a faith that is personally meaningful, intellectually sound, socially relevant, and spiritually expansive. We are not ashamed to confess that "truth comes in small installments," to quote Universalist minister Clinton Lee Scott. Those modest and well-lived insights are sufficient to sustain a fulfilling existence.

TOM OWEN-TOWLE

I do not have a Personal Relationship with God.
    I've lost his phone number;
    he never answers his mail.

We did not, as young men,
    hang out on Wednesday nights,
    cigarettes dripping from our lips,
    at pool halls.

He is not there like an old neighbor
    to fix my broken lawn mower
    and hand me a soda
    on a blazing hot day.

When I rip my shin on a jutting shelf
    and cry out his name,
    he does not rush to me
    with Band-Aids and peroxide.

He does not, at times of vexation,
    when my world lies shattered,
    my relationships ruptured,
    my children insolent,
    my finances hopeless,
    come with soothing counsel to my side.

He does not take my requests
  like a long-distance dedication
  on America's Top Forty,
  or deliver within five business days
  or my money back
  on my catalog order—
    my business is not important to him.

I do not have a Personal Relationship with God.

But in quiet moments—
  in the familiar whistle
  of a red-winged blackbird on a cattail,
  or in spider webs glinting with dew
  in the grass of a clear sunrise,
  or the passing attention of an old cat—
    He/She/It/Whatever does not
    speak
      or do
       or answer
    but admits me to fleeting union
    with the Greater.

PATRICK MURFIN

Nothing is more curious than the self-satisfied dogmatism with which mankind at each period of its history cherishes the delusion of the finality of its existing modes of knowledge. . . . This dogmatic common sense is the death of philosophic adventure. The Universe is vast.

ALFRED NORTH WHITEHEAD

The devil once went for a walk with a friend. They saw a man ahead of them stoop down and pick up something from the ground.
"What did that man find?" asked the friend.
"A piece of truth," said the devil.
"Doesn't that disturb you?" asked the friend.
"No," said the devil. "I shall let him make a belief out of it."

FOLKTALE

The theology of doubt is the underlying theology of Unitarian Universalism. . . . It's a theology which keeps us from self-righteousness, but not action. . . . So let's cherish our doubts. They not only lead to larger truth, but they make us wise, keep us humble, and allow us to live together in love.

CHRISTINE ROBINSON

Out of the night that covers me,
    Black as the Pit from pole to pole,
I thank whatever gods may be
    For my unconquerable soul.

In the fell clutch of circumstance
    I have not winced nor cried aloud.
Under the bludgeonings of chance
    My head is bloody, but unbowed.

Beyond this place of wrath and tears
    Looms but the Horror of the shade,
And yet the menace of the years
    Finds, and shall find, me unafraid;

It matters not how strait the gate,
    How charged with punishments the scroll,
I am the master of my fate:
    I am the captain of my soul.

WILLIAM ERNEST HENLEY

My Humanist religion . . . prods me to consider the moral principles by which I should live. Humanist ethics, based on love and compassion for humankind and for nature, place the responsibility on humanity for shaping the destiny and future direction of the world. I am called to find my better self and to try to become the best person I can be. Humanism also makes me aware of the existence of moral dilemmas and the need to be very careful and intentional in my moral decision-making, for every decision and action has a consequence now and for the future. I am compelled by my own analysis of the world situation to become involved in service for the greater good of humanity, recognizing that things are changing so quickly that an open-ended approach to solving social problems is needed.

SARAH OELBERG

Our remedies oft in ourselves do lie
Which we ascribe to heaven; the fated sky
Gives us free scope, only doth backward pull
Our slow designs when we ourselves are dull.

WILLIAM SHAKESPEARE

The Really Interesting Things Happened 12 Billion Years Ago

This is nothing at all,
nothing more than the moon's reflection sprawled
across a rippled pond, a physical
manifestation of something distant. Meanwhile, the universe
spreads and thins. One day, it will likely reverse
itself, collapse, coerced
by gravity, but for now, I wait, wonder
about antimatter, the forces that tear stars asunder,
the astounding number
of photons trapped in black holes,
particles freezing
in deep space. Everything cools—
no time to question the wisdom of breathing.

MARY ZOLL

> though I have looked everywhere
> I can find nothing lowly
> in the universe. . . .

A.R. AMMONS

Humanism can be religious; indeed, the most meaningful and liveable kind of humanism is itself a religious way of understanding and living life. It offers a view of [people] and [their] place in the universe that is a religious philosophy . . . overarching and undergirding it all, there can be a haunting sense of wonder which never leaves one for whom life itself is a mystery and miracle. Where did we come from, why are we here, where are we going with all the effort, frustration, the grief, the joy? To be caught up in this sense of wider relatedness, to sense our being connected in live ways with all the world and everyone in it, is the heart dimension of religion, whatever its name.

PETER SAMSON

Of course truth is hard.
It is a rock.
Yet I do not think it will fall upon me
And crush me.
I do not think they can hammer it to bits
And stone me.

Help me place the rock in the strong current
Of these rushing waters.
I must climb upon it.
I must know how truth feels.

When I plunge naked
Into the bright depth of these waters,
I must know how truth feels.
When I am swept by the cold fury of these waters,
I must know, with my whole being, how truth feels.
I shall remember how truth feels.

I praise the rock.
I praise the river.
I fear the drought
More than death by water.

BARBARA ROHDE

An honest "No" is a glorious statement.
Doubt is the expression of faith in the intelligence and imagination of
humanity.
Doubt is the expression of humility about the capacity for errors and
mistakes.
Doubt is the expression of wisdom when popular and rewarding
truths are wrong.
Doubt is the expression of confidence that knowledge can always be
improved.
Doubt is the expression of courage in confronting the dangerous and
destructive.

Doubt is the expression of hope that a better world is waiting for the
    future.
Doubt is the expression of harmony with the unceasingly changing
    universe.
Doubt is the expression of concern for the proper integration of
    thought and experience.
It is not evil, but good, an intrinsic element of faith.

DAVID RANKIN

Long long ago, it seemed so simple. The universe was a three-storied
apartment house, with heaven on the top floor, full of gods and stars;
earth in the middle, full of people and animals and plants, and hell in
the basement, full of terrible and scary things. God had nothing else
to do but sit up there watching us. We were the center of attention.
We were his people.

Then came Copernicus. He said that the sun did not move around
the earth at all, but was a fixed star. He said it was the earth and us
on it that did the moving, and worse, that the earth was just one of
the planets that so moved, one among many, and not at the center of
anything at all. . . .

In the last few decades we have been entering a new vision of the universe as radical and revolutionary as the Copernican changeover, and we still have not worked out what it all means, either in theology or in our view of what humanity is and what we ought to do with our lives.

Judith Walker-Riggs

I think everybody knows what it's like to be Thomas. . . . Thomas is a patron saint for those of us who are trying to live a critical faith. He is not satisfied with other people's accounts: he wants to know by experience. He wants his religion to be his own. He wants to touch the truth for himself, and until then, maybe even in spite of himself, he says he will not believe. In this way Thomas approached religion *critically*. But Thomas was not an unbeliever. He did not decide that the others were deluded, . . . that all this talk about the kingdom of God was just so much magical language for lesser minds. Thomas's critical instinct did not destroy his concern for the life that might be, but isn't yet, in the world. Thomas's religion is a critical *faith*.

Chris Walton

Now Thomas, one of the Twelve, called the Twin, was not with them when Jesus came. So the other disciples told him, "We have seen the Lord." But he said to them," Unless I see in his hands the mark of the nails, and place my finger into the mark of the nails, and place my hand into his side, I will never believe."

JOHN 20:24–25

Cherish your doubts, for doubt is the attendant of truth.
Doubt is the key to the door of knowledge; it is the servant of discovery.

A belief which may not be questioned binds us to error, for there is
    incompleteness and imperfection in every belief.
Doubt is the touchstone of truth; it is an acid which eats away the
    false.

Let no one fear for the truth, that doubt may consume it; for doubt is
    a testing of belief.
The truth stands boldly and unafraid; it is not shaken by the testing.

For truth, if it be truth, arises from each testing stronger, more secure.
Those that would silence doubt are filled with fear; their houses are
    built on shifting sands.

But those who fear not doubt, and know its use, are founded on rock.
They shall walk in the light of growing knowledge; the work of their
    hands shall endure.

Therefore let us not fear doubt, let us rejoice in its help:
It is to the wise as a staff to the blind; doubt is the attendant of truth.

ROBERT T. WESTON

The universe does not
revolve around you.
The stars and planets spinning
through the ballroom of space
dance with one another
quite outside of your small life.
You cannot hold gravity
or seasons; even air and water
inevitably evade your grasp.
Why not, then, let go?

You could move through time
like a shark through water,
neither restless nor ceasing,
absorbed in and absorbing

the native element.
Why pretend you can do otherwise?
The world comes in at every pore,
mixes in your blood before
breath releases you into
the world again. Did you think
the fragile boundary of your skin
could build a wall?

Listen. Every molecule is humming
its particular pitch.
Of course you are a symphony.
Whose tune do you think
the planets are singing
as they dance?

LYNN UNGAR

The practice of humanism is service; service to a world much wider than our own beliefs, our own culture, our own comfort. And it is when we are engaged in that service that our ministry will speak for us, and tell the world in no uncertain terms what humanism is. Let us lift high the light that is within us, the light that we are together, and let it shine.

KENDYL GIBBONS

I must live my own way,
Refusing all that binds.
I must know my own mind
Among all other minds.
I must do my own deeds,
And in whatever lands.
I will know my own hands
Among all other hands.

I must forsake the crowds,
And walk with lonely fools,
To seek for my own face
In bleak, deserted pools.
I must leave worn old roads,
To walk on hillside grass,
To follow my own feet
Out in the wilderness.

KENNETH L. PATTON

Say not, "I have found the truth," but rather, "I have found a truth."
Say not, "I have found the path of the soul." Say rather, "I have met
the soul walking upon my path."

KAHLIL GIBRAN

During the years of my formal education, I particularly valued that Humanism honors reason and encourages integrity. I liked that it invited me to think for myself, to explore, challenge, and doubt; to approach the important questions of life with an openness to new ideas and different perspectives; and then to test these ideas against reality, filter new knowledge through my own active mind, and believe according to the evidence. Humanism provided me with the "tools" I would use to pursue the "free and responsible search for truth and meaning." It invited me to ask about each idea, "Is it reasonable and responsible to believe this? Does it make sense in terms of what is known about the world and the universe?" This is not to suggest that we do not also learn and gain insights from intuition, hunches, flashes of inspiration, even emotion or unexplainable experiences—we do. But when making important decisions that will affect ourselves and others, it behooves us to test our perceptions against reality.

SARAH OELBERG

All truly wise thoughts have been thought already thousands of times; but to make them truly ours, we must think them over again honestly, till they take firm root in our personal experience.

JOHANN WOLFGANG VON GOETHE

It is astonishing what force, purity and wisdom it requires for a human being to keep clear of falsehoods.

Margaret Fuller

Pray with me now,
if you will.
I think
we need
to pray.

Pray with me now.
Not out to some great intervener,
a handsome stranger
coming to the rescue.
You don't have to barter your soul,
your mind, your free and restless spirit.
Pray with me now.

We need to pray loudly sometimes,
giving voice in word or gesture
to the urgent fires within our hearts.
Screaming out, "Why this?"
"How long?"

Screaming out for help, for courage.
Outrage rumbles through our veins
and the pulse of our prayer is ragged.

Pray with me now,
if you will,
I think
we need
to pray.

We need to pray softly sometimes,
our silent bodies held still,
a quiet hope rising to the wind,
blowing about the world in wonder.

Pray with me now.
Pray silently or out loud.

Our very prayers are an answer,
the pulse of life, of hope,
in our oh so human hearts.
May our prayers be heard.

THERESA NOVAK

Far from having nothing to say, religious liberals have to proclaim, over and over again, against both religious and secular adversaries, the good news that the future remains open and the Fates are not in control.

GENE REEVES

Humanism is a celebration and a promise; it celebrates the integrity of human reason, responsibility and compassion, and it promises a satisfying lifestyle that can be counted on. No more deprecation of the human condition; rather, an opportunity to remain true to ourselves by having both feet in this world and responding to the challenges of existence with excitement and pragmatic service to others. Humanism is religion come of age; at long last we humans can live dignified lives, finite creatures though we may be. At long last, men, women and children can find ultimate fulfillment through bringing out the best in humanity for the sake of humanity.

BEVERLEY EARLES

Let me keep the doors of my mind open
  for the possible knock of some vagrant truth.

Let me swing wide the shuttered windows of my heart
  that perchance some winged messenger of love light upon my sill.

CLINTON LEE SCOTT

Our age is retrospective. It builds the sepulchers of the fathers. It writes biographies, histories, and criticism. The foregoing generations beheld God and nature face to face; we, through their eyes. Why should not we also enjoy an original relation to the universe? Why should not we have a poetry and philosophy of insight and not of tradition, and a religion by revelation to us, and not the history of theirs? Embosomed for a season in nature, whose floods of life stream around and through us, and invite us by the powers they supply, to action proportioned to nature, why should we grope among the dry bones of the past, or put the living generation into masquerade out of its faded wardrobe? The sun shines today also. There is more wool and flax in the fields. There are new lands, new men, new thoughts. Let us demand our own works and laws and worship.

RALPH WALDO EMERSON

Humanism in religion is the shifting of emphasis from God to [humans], making the enrichment of human life . . . the object of our allegiance. . . . And somehow within us is a voice which urgently calls us. It is the life-urge. It is the aspiration after better things. It is [humans at their] best and bravest. It is what many call divine. Some even call it God. In any case, it is religion.

JOHN DIETRICH

The test of a first-rate intelligence is the ability to hold two opposed ideas in the mind at the same time, and still retain the ability to function.

F. SCOTT FITZGERALD

Our heritage rejects authoritarian religion and its negative view of human beings. Our forebears claimed a more positive view. They said we are born with capacities for good and evil and possess a whole array of gifts and abilities. Our powers can be used in the service of all sorts of values, but the choice is in our hands. Chief among the human gifts we celebrate is the capacity to think and to reason. Our affirmation of reason is part and parcel of our affirmation of the essential goodness and worthiness of human life. We replaced outside authorities with the inner authority of conscience and reason.

Rebecca Parker

I call that mind free which jealously guards its intellectual rights and powers, which does not content itself with a passive or hereditary faith, which opens itself to light whencesoever it may come, which receives new truth as an angel from heaven.

William Ellery Channing

As we daily see men arriving at opposite conclusions from the same premises it seems to me doubtful policy to speak too positively on any complex subject however much a man may feel convinced of the truth of his own conclusions.

Charles Darwin

Evolutionary versions of each religion—Evolutionary Buddhism, Evolutionary Christianity, Evolutionary Islam, Evolutionary Judaism, Evolutionary Hinduism, and more—are emerging. Why is this happening? Because adherents of each tradition have discovered the same thing: *Religious insights and perspective freed from the narrowness of their time and place of origin are more comprehensive and grounded in measurable reality than anyone could have possibly dreamed before.*

MICHAEL DOWD

If you want the truth, I'll tell you the truth:
Listen to the secret sound, the real sound, which is
    inside you.

KABIR

Older religious thought was much concerned with the question of personal immortality. We frankly admit that from the strictly scientific point of view the future is beyond our ken. We may think we find certain "intimations of immortality." Have we not all had moments of illumination when "eternity" becomes not a period of time but a quality of existence? But after all, our primary interest is with the present life. And we are none the less spiritual for that.

But if we no longer visualize ourselves either as "walking golden streets" or "gnashing our teeth in outer darkness," are we then left with no incentives to higher living? For myself, I must say that I was never very keen on being an angel with a "crown upon my forehead" and "a harp within my hand." But the inner urge toward higher things is as strong as ever—yes, much stronger. No one who knows anything of the fierce joy of the conflict will worry much about his [or her] "reward in heaven."

If we live in a great impersonal universe with no friend to guide, it matters tremendously how we conduct ourselves, for we are actually the makers of human destiny. [Our responsibility] is to put beauty in place of ugliness, good in place of evil, laughter in place of tears; to dispel error with knowledge, hatred with love; displace strife and contention with peace and co-operation.

JOHN DIETRICH

SIXTH SOURCE

Spiritual teachings of Earth-centered traditions which celebrate the sacred circle of life and instruct us to live in harmony with the rhythms of nature

WHETHER WE ARE DIGGING a garden, or watching a lightning storm, or giving birth to a child, we come to know the mystery of life in our bodies in ways that words can evoke but never capture. Through embodying and naming the spirits of the world, we recognize and respect their presence, and honor their place in the changing seasons of our lives. For some of us, this is an intuitive personal practice; others of us make it part of our regular worship.

Earth-centered spirituality is rooted in ritual and devotional experience. As such, it offers an important counter-balance to the Protestant origins of Unitarian Universalist worship and practice. While there are many different Earth-centered traditions, they hold in common an embodied spirituality. Dancing and drumming and singing open us up to experience our connection with all life. With musical traditions that include chant and drone, percussion and wind instruments, Pagan ceremonies are often celebrated among us in smaller groups settings.

Earth-centered practices remind us all of how intimately connected we are to the cycles, seasons, and rhythms of nature. Some Unitarian Universalists who are Native American continue to be grounded in and practice the faith and rituals of their ancestors. UUs who are neo-Pagans, Druids, or Wiccans draw inspiration from a variety of sources. We may look back at the ancient Celtic roots of Paganism, or find meaning in Native American oral traditions. Inspiration may also come from sources that describe the Sacred Feminine and the Goddess, or from the worship of many gods and goddesses who represent the forces of nature.

As the environmental challenges of our time become ever more compelling and frightening, the grounding of earth-centered spirituality gives us strength for the political struggle to turn away from the policies and lifestyles which are destroying our planet.

Margot Adler, a Wiccan priestess and a Unitarian Universalist, says this about her spiritual path:

"I chose UUism because I need to live in balance. I can do all those wonderful, earth-centered spiritual things: sing under the stars, drum for hours, create moving ceremonies for the changes of seasons or the passage of time in the lives of men and women. But I also need to be a worldly, down-to-earth person in a complicated world—someone who believes oppression is real, that tragedies happen, that chaos happens, that not everything is for a purpose. Unitarian Universalism gives me a place to be at home with some of my closest friends: my doubts. Of course, there are many rationalists within the earth-centered community, but somehow I feel more centered in this denomination. And I think, in turn, the Pagan community has brought to UUism the joy of ceremony, and a lot of creative and artistic ability that will leave the denomination with a richer liturgy and a bit more juice and mystery."

Indigenous religion, like Judaism, is not universal; it's based on place. Native American nations and cultures have their sacred mountains, their sacred spots, just as Jews have the land of Israel. Indigenous traditions don't get involved in proselytizing because they don't assume that other people should be part of their religious tradition. This is a huge notion, because if you don't proselytize, then how can you have a religious war?

MARGOT ADLER

We are called to define the religious and spiritual dimensions of the ecological crisis confronting the world and to preach the gospel of a world where each is part of all, where everyone is sacred, and every place is holy ground, where all are children of the same great love, all embarked on the same journey, all destined for the same end.

DAVID BUMBAUGH

There is something of the pagan in us all—something that responds to the great spinning Earth that calls us to worship daily, that fills our soul, that heals our spirit, that enables us to greet the new day and the new season not with dread but with anticipation.

RICHARD GILBERT

In the esoteric Judaism of the Cabalah, the Deep Self is named the Neshama, from the root of *Shmh*, "to hear or listen": the Neshama is She Who Listens, the soul who inspires and guides us.

STARHAWK

We Indians think of the earth and the whole universe as a never-ending circle, and in this circle man is just another animal. The buffalo and the coyote are our brothers; the birds, our cousins. Even the tiniest ant, even a louse, even the smallest flower you can find—they are all relatives.

JENNY LEADING CLOUD

I believe a leaf of grass is no less than the journey-work of the stars,
And the pismire is equally perfect, and a grain of sand, and the egg of
    the wren.
And the tree-toad is a chef-d'oeuvre for the highest,
And the running blackberry would adorn the parlors of heaven,
And the narrowest hinge in my hand puts to scorn all machinery,
And the cow crunching with depress'd head surpasses any statue,
And a mouse is miracle enough to stagger sextillions of infidels.

WALT WHITMAN

What would the world be, once bereft
Of wet and of wildness? Let them be left,
O let them be left, wildness and wet;
Long live the weeds and the wilderness yet.

GERARD MANLEY HOPKINS

When thoughts
Of the last bitter hour come like a blight
Over thy spirit, and sad images
Of the stern agony, and shroud, and pall,
And breathless darkness, and the narrow house,
Make thee to shudder, and grow sick at heart;—
Go forth, under the open sky, and list
To Nature's teachings, while from all around—
Earth and her waters, and the depths of air,—
Comes a still voice. . . .

WILLIAM CULLEN BRYANT

The wheel of the year turns. Seasons change. Darkness gives way to light, which wanes into darkness. Birth and death and birth and death and birth. Each has its season, and each season is a necessary part of the whole. It is the way of all nature. Let us embrace it with faith.

PAT MONTLEY

> May goddess flow again through
> the dried-up riverbeds of human minds.
> May she well up once more from the
> blocked springs of human hearts.
> May she dance with courage in
> office blocks and railway stations and
> through virtual space around the world,
> dissolving hierarchies and creating
> at last a genuine deep equality for
> all members of the human race.

JOCELYN CHAPLIN

Mother Earth, we are gathered here this morning to bask in your beauty and reflect on your place in our lives. Too often we forget how you feed us, whisper in our ears, and sprinkle our sleep with dreams. Help us to remember that through you we are all joyfully connected.

We pray for your presence among us, Great Mother. Our burdens can be great, and we feel alone. Our hands have not felt the touch of another, and our hearts long for reconciliation, compassion, and understanding.

Now, on this day, we open our hearts to you and to one another. We breathe in your love, and feel that we are worthy of love. We feel your touch, and know that we are touched. We pray for the well-being of all creatures on the earth, for your spirit, Mother Earth, lives within, and connects us all. Thank you for the many gifts and blessings in our lives. As we give love, may we also receive love. Amen.

SHARON DITTMAR

The bare vastness of the Hopi landscape emphasizes the visual impact of every plant, every rock, every arroyo. Nothing is overlooked or taken for granted. Each ant, each lizard, each lark is imbued with great value simply because the creature is there, simply because the creature is alive in a place where any life at all is precious. Stand on the mesa edge at Walpai and look west over the bare distances toward the pale blue outlines of the San Francisco peaks where the ka'tsina spirits reside. So little lies between you and the sky. So little lies between you and the earth. One look and you know that simply to survive is a great triumph, that every possible resource is needed, every possible ally—even the most humble insect or reptile. You realize you will be speaking with all of them if you intend to last out the year. Thus it is that the Hopi elders are grateful to the landscape for aiding them in their quest as spiritual people.

LESLIE MARMON SILKO

As a being in an active relation to the world [one] comes into a spiritual relation with it by not living for himself alone, but feeling himself one with all life that comes within his reach. . . . He injures and destroys life only under a necessity which he cannot avoid, and never from thoughtlessness. So far as he is a free man he uses every opportunity of tasting the blessedness of being able to assist life and avert from it suffering and destruction.

ALBERT SCHWEITZER

Before I came I was in the birdsong
announcing dawn,
in globes of dew
on needles of the spruce
dropping onto fallow fields.

I could hear gulls
spread sound over the sea,
colored blue by dawn light,
and feel swelling water
bounce off the ocean floor.

There in shafts of light
the bones of my ancestors
began to drum an echo,
and to that beat
stone pounded stone upon the shore.

Out of the rock came life,
animals ground seeds;
I inhaled life
in the first breath
that blew through a reed.
My flesh moved
with other hands drawing
rhythm from a skin drum;

knowing hunger in the reach
of an empty bowl.
I wore my beads
and danced on earth's soft face,
gave life, helped children to their feet,
learned from smooth stones
to question my uneven edges.

For a time it is all mine,
until my bones form
instruments for the coming dancers
whose song, whose indecipherable words,
my spirit will come to understand.

JACQUELINE BEAUREGARD

May we make space every day to remember what the ancients knew, what has been woven into the tissue of our hearts since the evolution of humankind—that the universe is a miraculous wonder to be celebrated and that a miracle that happens every day is no less a miracle.

ANNE PEEK

This earthen chalice was born of clay and water,
    the flesh and blood of Gaia;
Given form by the hand of the potter,
    set by the bonding fire of the kiln.
As we touch the flame to her lips,
    joining fire and air,
May her light remind us of that unity
    of earth, air, fire, and water,
    of plant and animal, human and mineral,
    that we and the earth are one.

ED A. LANE

Like a quetzal plume, a fragrant flower,
friendship sparkles
Like heron plumes, it weaves itself into finery.
Our song is a bird calling out like a jingle
how beautiful you make it sound!
Here, among flowers that enclose us,
Among flowery boughs you are singing.

AZTEC POEM

If you can appreciate the Earth, you can appreciate the beauty of yourself. The same creator created both. And if I learned to take care of that I'll also take care of myself and help take care of others.

RACHEL BAGBY

Nestled in a hillside on the snow-crusted high plains, embedded in the starlit ebony of the winter solstice, my Unitarian Fellowship heralds the coming days of growing light that will become spring. Spaced evenly by holding hands, we sing "Lord of the Dance" and weave a line that passes through and around itself. The only music is our voices; the only rule is that the line remain unbroken. The bounded chaos is a model of life and pure celebration.

JEFF LOCKWOOD

Deep peace of the running way to you.
Deep peace of the flower air to you.
Deep peace of the quiet earth to you.
Deep peace of the shining stars to you.
Deep peace of the infinite peace to you.

GAELIC RUNES, ADAPTED

The earth is a living, conscious being. In company with cultures of many different times and places, we name these things as sacred: air, fire, water, and earth.

Whether we see them as the breath, energy, blood and body of the Mother, or as the blessed gifts of a Creator, or as symbols of the interconnected systems that sustain life, we know that nothing can live without them.

To call these things sacred is to say that they have a value beyond their usefulness for human ends, that they themselves become the standards by which our acts, our economics, our laws and our purposed must be judged. . . .

To honor the sacred is to create conditions in which nourishment, sustenance, habitat, knowledge, freedom, and beauty can thrive. To honor the sacred is to make love possible.

STARHAWK

All the matter of the Earth was created by the Grandmother Star that preceded our Sun. She fashioned the carbon and nitrogen and all the elements that would later become all the bodies and things of Earth. And when she was done with her immense creativity, she exploded in celebration of her achievement, sharing her riches with the universe and enabling our birth.

BRIAN SWIMME

Isis, Astarte, Diana, Hecate,
Demeter, Kali, Inanna

We chanted,
a roomful of women
away for the weekend
for Goddess time.

I was needing a Goddess,
and thinking of waning moons,
so I had put a smooth, black stone
in my pocket.

We chanted,
with the stone in my pocket,
with the stone in my hand,
my Goddess this weekend
was Kali, but did I dare?

We chanted.
Unbidden she came to me.
The name on my lips,
the sound from my belly,
was Kali,
destroyer of demons.

Kali — not Hecate.
Kali — not Inanna.
It wasn't a matter of daring;
the moment would not be refused.

Not long after,
the demon-built walls
around my life
began to fall.

I embraced the pain
and thanked this Goddess,
treasuring that black stone
as I sang my new life into being.

MARY WELLEMEYER

Praise the earth, all its creatures
Praise the earth, all plants and minerals
Praise the earth, all rivers and mountains
Praise the earth, all deserts and forests

Praise her, from whom we come
Praise her, in whom we live

She causes the nesting birds to return
    and the bulbs to awaken and send forth shoots
She causes the grain to rise up
    and the rice to fill its paddies
She causes green to green, and red to redden,
    and the fruits of vine and tree to ripen

The winds and clouds are her robes,
    and the rainbow her veil
She sings to the stars and moon by night
Her sister planets sing with her
Together they dance around the sun

Do not test her patience
For at her core she is molten
Her passion will overcome you
With miasma and flame

Tread on her gently, treat her with honor
Treat her with honor,
        as a child its grandmother

Praise her, from whom we come
Praise her, in whom we live

JANET C. BUSH

The Hopis say that we all began together, that each race went on a journey to learn its own road to power, and changed; that now is the time for us to return, to put the pieces of the puzzle back together, to make the circle whole. Through our differences, we complete each other. Together, we become a new whole. Mystery is vision.

STARHAWK

Our universe is a universe of surprise. We put our confidence not in our human egos but in the power that gathered the stars and knit the first living cells together. Remember that you are here through the creativity of others. You have awakened in a great epic of being, a drama that is 15 to 20 billion years in the making. The intelligence that

ignited the first minds, the care that spaced the notes of the nightin-
gale, the power that heaved all 100 billion galaxies across the sky now
awakens as you, too, and permeates your life no less thoroughly.

Brian Swimme

May clarity grow within me
Open my eyes to life's many wonders
May I feel the pulse of all creation within me
Open my spirit to Awareness
Fill my heart with deeper Understanding
May my life be of service to Earth and the Goddess

Open my ears to the needs of those around me
Make my hands strong, sure, & gentle in your service
May I remember always, the Goddess works through me

Abby Willowroot

We are of the stars,
the dust of the explosions
cast across space.

We are of the earth:
we breathe and live in the breath
of ancient plants and beasts. . . .

We are a part
of the great circle of humanity
gathered around the fire, the
    hearth, the altar.

JOY ATKINSON

In the ever-shifting water of the river of this life
I was swimming, seeking comfort; I was wrestling waves to find
A boulder I could cling to, a stone to hold me fast
Where I might let the fretful water of this river 'round me pass

And so I found an anchor, a blessed resting place
A trusty rock I called my savior, for there I would be safe
From the river and its dangers, and I proclaimed my rock divine
And I prayed to it "protect me" and the rock replied

God is a river, not just a stone
God is a wild, raging rapids
And a slow, meandering flow

God is a deep and narrow passage
And a peaceful, sandy shoal
God is the river, swimmer
So let go

Still I clung to my rock tightly with conviction in my arms
Never looking at the stream to keep my mind from thoughts of harm
But the river kept on coming, kept on tugging at my legs
Till at last my fingers faltered, and I was swept away

So I'm going with the flow now, these relentless twists and bends
Acclimating to the motion, and a sense of being led
And this river's like my body now, it carries me along
Through the ever-changing scenes and by the rocks that sing this song.

PETER MAYER

I do not see a delegation for the four-footed. I see no seat for the
eagles. We forget and we consider ourselves superior, but we are after
all a mere part of the Creation. And we must continue to understand
where we are. And we stand between the mountain and the ant,
somewhere and there only, as part and parcel of the Creation. It is
our responsibility, since we have been given the minds to take care of
these things.

OREN LYONS

Blessed are the heavens,
for they declare the power of creation.
Blessed is the earth, our beloved home,
for she is a planet of plenitude.
Blessed are the waters thereon,
for they gave rise to living things.
Blessed is the land,
for it is the source of life abundant.
Blessed is the air we breathe,
for it fires us to life and love.
Blessed are the beasts of the field,
for they are glorious to behold.
Blessed are the birds of the air,
for they carve a graceful arc in the sky.
Blessed are the mountains and the seas and the valleys,
for their variety makes rich our habitat.
Blessed are the fields of grain, the orchards of fruit,
for they give sustenance, asking nothing in return.
Blessed are the dwellers on earth,
for they cherish the privilege of living upon it.
Blessed are they who protect the earth and all her creatures,
from the plants of the field to the trees of the forest,
for their reward shall be harmony with the web of existence.
Rejoice, and be glad,
for the earth and her people are one.

RICHARD GILBERT

I go among trees and sit still.
All my stirring becomes quiet
around me like circles on water.

WENDELL BERRY

All creatures go forth from me and all return unto Me; thus rise and
set my immense days and nights.

BHAGAVAD GITA 9:7

I pledge allegiance to the earth and all life:
the fields and streams, the mountains and seas,
the forests and deserts, the air and soil,
all species and reserves, habitats and environments;
one world, one creation, one home, indivisible for all,
affected by pollution anywhere, depleted by any waste,
endangered by greedy consumption, degraded by faithlessness;
protected, preserved by reducing, reusing, recycling:
With conservation and reverence,
the great gift renewed for all generations to come.

VERN BARNET

Is not the sky a father, and the earth a mother, and are not all living things with feet or wings or roots their children?

BLACK ELK

All creatures of the earth and sky,
come, kindred, lift your voices high, Alleluia, Alleluia!
Bright burning sun with golden beam,
soft shining moon with silver gleam: Alleluia, Alleluia
Alleluia, Alleluia, Alleluia!

Swift rushing wind so wild and strong,
white clouds that sail in heav'n along, Alleluia, Alleluia!
Fair rising morn in praise rejoice,
high stars of evening find a voice: Alleluia, Alleluia
Alleluia, Alleluia, Alleluia!

Cool flowing water, pure and clear,
make music for all life to hear, Alleluia, Alleluia!
Dance, flame of fire, so strong and bright,
and bless us with your warmth and light: Alleluia, Alleluia
Alleluia, Alleluia, Alleluia!

Embracing earth, you, day by day,
bring forth your blessings on our way, Alleluia, Alleluia!
All herbs and fruits that richly grow,
let them the glory also show: Alleluia, Alleluia,
Alleluia, Alleluia, Alleluia!

All you of understanding heart,
forgiving others, take your part, Alleluia, Alleluia!
Let all things now the holy bless,
and worship God in humbleness: Alleluia, Alleluia,
Alleluia, Alleluia, Alleluia!

FRANCIS OF ASSISI (ATTRIBUTED)

A NOTE ON MULTICULTURAL READINGS

A vision for Unitarian Universalism in a multicultural world:

With humility and courage born of our history, we are called as Unitarian Universalists to build the Beloved Community, where all souls are welcome as blessings, and the human family lives whole and reconciled.

> —Leadership Council of the Unitarian Universalist Association of Congregations, October 2008

One of the great strengths of Unitarian Universalism, embodied in our six Sources, is our belief that spiritual wisdom speaks with many voices. This understanding is the key to welcoming all souls into our faith communities as blessings. Every new person we encounter has something to teach us. Values such as love, peace, compassion, and justice are expressed in every culture and tradition all over the world, in beautifully and powerfully different ways. Taken together, these expressions illuminate the various facets of these ideas, giving them nuance and depth. But only if we allow them to.

Looking for commonalities is the relatively easy part of forming a multicultural community. True multiculturalism, however, means being humble and brave enough to explore our different perspectives, experiences, traditions, and values while staying in relationship. It means bringing our whole selves to the table and inviting others to do the same, not just the parts that "fit in." It means being willing to be changed.

None of us feels welcomed as a blessing if we are asked to leave parts of ourselves behind, if we are constantly asked to translate our beliefs, perspectives, and spiritual questions into the language and frame of reference of the majority. We do not feel that we are recognized for the gifts we have to offer if our interactions and relationships leave no room for mutual transformation.

Learning from and about each other helps us practice true hospitality. When we share our cultural traditions with one another in worship, we can offer this welcoming message: "We value your rich tradition and worldview so much that we are committed to learning about it."

Often readings carry cultural resonances and meanings that extend beyond the words alone. If you use these readings in worship, in religious education, in small group ministry (and I hope you will), I encourage you to consider it part of your standard preparation to research some of their context. Learn and share as much as you can about the authors or speakers, their stories, their cultural and historical contexts, and the significance attached to what they've said or written.

If you use the Internet for your research, pay particular attention to websites and online books developed or published by cultural organizations and academic institutions. Personal websites are not reliable.

Once you learn more about a reading from a cultural tradition different from your own, you may become aware of its deeper meaning within its own context. For example, consider the following reading by Mohandas K. Gandhi:

> Non-violence is like radium in its action. An infinitesimal quantity of it embedded in a malignant growth acts continuously, silently and ceaselessly till it has transformed the whole mass of the diseased tissue into a healthy one. Similarly, even a little of true non-violence acts in a silent, subtle, unseen way and leavens the whole society.

Most people know the rough outline of Gandhi's story and that he is associated with the ethic of non-violence. But how many of us who are not Hindu, Buddhist, or Jain fully understand the implications of *ahimsa*, the sacred vow that was the foundation of Gandhi's activism? The depth and nuance of *ahimsa* cannot be conveyed by the English word *nonviolence*. With a brief Internet search, you can learn about Gandhi's understanding of *ahimsa*, congruencies and differences between *ahimsa* and Unitarian Universalist affirmations of the worth and dignity of every person and the interdependent web, Gandhi's legacy for activists Albert Schweitzer and Martin Luther King Jr., and explanations of *ahimsa* as the philosophical basis for Hindu practices like yoga and vegetarianism that have become popular in the West.

Unitarian Universalists are a people engaged in the perpetual search for truth and meaning. What any one of us knows and has experienced is only one piece of the truth. Let us open ourselves to what we can learn from each other, as well as from those we have yet to meet.

INDEX OF FIRST LINES

CREDITS

Selections appear on page numbers in bold.

ADLER   "Vibrant, Juicy, Contemporary: or, Why I Am a UU Pagan" (interview with Margot Adler) (**129**), in *The World*, Sep/Oct 1996.

AMMONS   From "Still" (**107**), copyright © 1965 by A.R. Ammons, from *Collected Poems 1951–1971* by A.R. Ammons. Used by permission of W.W. Norton & Company, Inc.

ANGELOU   From "Thank You, Lord" (**83**), copyright © 1978 by Maya Angelou, from *And Still I Rise* by Maya Angelou. Used by permission of Random House, Inc.

ARAMAIC PRAYER OF JESUS   "O Birther! Father-Mother of the Cosmos" (p. 41:18 l.) (**82**), from *Prayers of the Cosmos: Meditations on the Aramaic Words of Jesus* by Neil Douglas-Klotz, copyright © 1990 by Neil Douglas-Klotz, Foreword © 1990 by Matthew Fox. Reprinted by permission of HarperCollins Publishers.

ARGOW   "An Eternal Verity" (**48**) by W. Waldemar W. Argow, in *Singing the Living Tradition*, 1993.

ATKINSON   From "The Womb of Stars" (**144**) by Joy Atkinson. Reprinted with permission of author.

Augustine of Hippo   Prayer (**84**) by Augustine of Hippo, in *Via Christi: An Introduction to the Study of Missions* by Louise Manning Hodgkins, 1901.

Aztec Poem   Aztec poem (**137**), in *The Book of Love*, edited by Andrew M. Greeley and Mary G. Durkin, 2002.

Baal Shem Tov   Wisdom tale (**79**), in *Wise Words: Jewish Thoughts and Stories Through the Ages* collected by Jessica Gribetz, 1997.

Baba   Selection (**47**) by Neem Karoli Baba, in *Simple Wicca: A Simple Wisdom Book* by Michele Morgan, 2000.

Bagavad Gita   Bagavad Gita 9:7 (**148**) in *The Bagavad Gita: Anotated and Explained*, trans. by Shri Purohit Swami, 2001.

Bagby   Selection (**138**) by Rachel Bagby, in *Feminism & Ecology: An Introduction* by Mary Mellor, 1997.

Ballou   *Autobiography of Adin Ballou, 1803–1890* (**27**) by Adin Ballou, 1896.

Barnet   "I Pledge Allegiance to the Earth and All Life" (**148**) by Vern Barnet. Reprinted with permission of author.

Barnwell   "We Are . . ." (**38**) by Ysaye Barnwell, © 1991 Barnwell's Notes Publishing (BMI). Reprinted with permission of author.

Barth   Selection (**51**) by Karl Barth, in *True Prayer: An Invitation to Christian Spirituality* by Kenneth Leech, 1980.

BEAUREGARD   "From Song to Echo" (**135**) by Jacqueline Beauregard. Reprinted with permission of the author.

BELLETINI   "When to Speak, When to Keep Silence" (**31**), in *Sonata for Voice and Silence* by Mark Belletini, 2008. Reprinted with permission of author.

BERRY   From "I go among trees and sit still" (**148**), in *A Timbered Choir: The Sabbath Poems 1979–1997* by Wendell Berry, 1999. Reprinted with permission of Counterpoint Press.

BLACK ELK   *Black Elk Speaks* (**18**, **149**) by John Gneisenau Niehardt, 1932.

BLAKE   "Eternity" (**20**) by William Blake, in *Americans' Favorite Poems: The Favorite Poems Project Anthology*, edited by Robert Pinsky and Maggie Dietz, 2000.

BOWENS-WHEATLEY   "To Keep One's Soul" (**47**) by Marjorie Bowens-Wheatley, in *Christian Voices in Unitarian Universalism*, edited by Kathleen Rolenz, 2006.

BRIHDARANYAKA UPANISADA 1:3:28   Brihdaranyaka Upanisada 1:3:28 (**68**), reprinted by permission of World Prayers, www.worldprayers. org.

BROWN   Selection (**15**) by Olympia Brown, from a sermon preached at the Universalist Church, Racine, Wisconsin, September 12, 1920.

Bryant   From "Thanatopsis" (**131**) in *Thanatopsis and Other Poems* by William Cullen Bryant, 1884.

Buddha   Dhammapada 223 (**29**), in *Pali Text and Translation with Stories in Brief and Notes* by Nârada Thera, 2002. "The Buddha's First Sermon" (**62**), excerpt from "The Buddha's First Sermon," in *The Wisdom Bible,* edited by Sanderson Beck, published by World Peace Communications and at http://san.beck.org/Buddha.html. Reprinted with permission of Sanderson Beck. Dhammapada 183 (**62**), a free rendering.

Buddhist parable   Buddhist parable (**61**), as retold by Kathleen Rolenz.

Buechner   *Wishful Thinking* (**11**) by Frederick Buechner, 1993.

Bumbaugh   Selection (**129**) by David Bumbaugh, in *A Chosen Faith: An Introduction to Unitarian Universalism*, Rev. ed., by John Buehrens and Forrest Church, 1998. Reprinted with permission of author.

Bush   Prayer (**142**) by Janet C. Bush. Reprinted with permission of author.

Butts   "My Psalm" (**86**) by Roger Butts, in *How We Are Called*, edited by Mary Benard and Kirstie Anderson, 2003.

Carretto   *Letters from the Desert* (**6**) by Carlo Carretto, trans. by Rose Mary Hancock, 2002.

CASEBOLT   Chalice lighting (**52**) by Beth Casebolt. Reprinted with permission of author.

CHANNING   "Spiritual Freedom" (**122**), in *The Complete Works of W.E. Channing* by William Ellery Channing, 1884.

CHAPLIN   Prayer (**132**) by Jocelyn Chaplin, in *Prayers for a Thousand Years*, edited by Elizabeth Roberts and Elias Amidon,1999.

CHINOOK PSALTER   From Chinook psalter (**71**), in *Earth Prayers from Around the World: 365 Prayers, Poems, and Invocations for Honoring the Earth*, edited by Elizabeth Roberts and Elias Amidon, 1991.

CONFUCIUS   "The Great Learning" (**68**) by Confucius, in *The Chinese Classics,* Vol. 1, trans. by James Legge, 1861.

CROSBY   Selection (**51**) by Greta Crosby, in *A Chosen Faith: An Introduction to Unitarian Universalism*, Rev. ed., by John Buehrens and Forrest Church, 1998. Reprinted with permission of author.

DALAI LAMA   *Words of Wisdom from the Dalai Lama: Quotes by His Holiness* (**64**) by the Dalai Lama, 2005.

DARWIN   Letter 5500 from Charles Darwin to E. Haeckel (**122**), in *The Correspondence of Charles Darwin*, Vol. 15, 1867.

DAVIES   Prayer (**89**) by A. Powell Davies, in *Prayers for Today*, edited by Herbert Vetter, 2004.

DAY   *Loaves and Fishes* (**28**) by Dorothy Day, 1972.

Deuteronomy   Deuteronomy 15:7–11 (**29**), New Revised Standard Version. Deuteronomy 6: 4–6 (**77**), New International Version. Deuteronomy 30:19 (**78**), World English Bible.

Dietrich   Selection (**121**) by John Dietrich, in "Religious Humanism: The Past We Inherit; The Future We Create," *Humanism Today*, Vol. 12. "Humanism" (pamphlet) (**123**) by John Dietrich, 1934.

Dillard   *For the Time Being* (**19**) by Annie Dillard, 2000.

Dittmar   Prayer (**133**) by Sharon Dittmar. Reprinted with permission of author.

Dogen   *Eihei Dogen: Mystical Realist* (**63**) by Dogen, 2004.

Dowd   *Thank God for Evolution* (**123**) by Michael Dowd, 2008.

Earles   Selection (**119**) by Beverley Earles. Reprinted with permission of author.

Edelman   From prayer (**37**), in *Guide My Feet* by Marian Wright Edelman © 1995 Marian Wright Edelman. Reprinted by permission of Beacon Press.

Einstein   *Cosmic Religion, with other Opinions and Aphorisms* (**18**) by Albert Einstein, 1931. *The World as I See It* (**20**) by Albert Einstein, 2011.

Ellis   Selection (**85**) by Elizabeth Ellis, in "Unitarian Universalist Views of God" (pamphlet), edited by Paul B. Rasor, 2001.

EMERSON   "Circles" (**5**), "Journal, 1838" (**12**), and "Nature" (**120**), in *The Complete Works of Ralph Waldo Emerson* by Ralph Waldo Emerson, 1903.

EXODUS   Exodus 3:4–5 (**6**), New Revised Standard Version.

FITZGERALD   "The Crack-up" (**121**), in *The Crack-Up* by F. Scott Fitzgerald, edited by Edmund Wilson, 1945.

FOLKTALE   Folktale (**104**), in *The Song of the Bird* by Anthony de Mello, copyright © 1982 by Anthony de Mello, S. J. Used by permission of Doubleday, a division of Random House, Inc.

FOUR BODHISATTVA VOWS   Four Bodhisattva Vows (**61**), in Boundless Way Zen Liturgy, 2007. Reprinted with permission.

FRANCIS OF ASSISI   Lyrics "All Creatures of the Earth and Sky" (**149**), attributed to Francis of Assisi.

FULLER   Letter (1838) (**7**), in *The Letters of Margaret Fuller, Vol. 1, 1817–1838*, 1983. "Summer on the Lakes" (**13**), in *At Home and Abroad or Things and Thoughts on America and Europe*, 1895. "Notes from Cambridge, Massachusetts (July 1842)" (**117**), in *Memoirs of Margaret Fuller Ossoli*, 1852.

GAELIC RUNES   Gaelic runes, adapted (**138**), in *Singing the Living Tradition*, 1993.

GANDHI   Selection (**30**) by Mohandas K. Gandhi, in *The Mind of Mahatma Gandhi*, compiled & edited by R. K. Prabhu & U. R. Rao, 1960. *An Autobiography: The Story of My Experiments With Truth* (**41**) by Mohandas K. Gandhi, 1957.

GANNET   From "The Morning Hangs a Signal" (**29**) by William Channing Gannet, in *Singing the Living Tradition*, 1993.

GIBBONS   From *The Sources Cantata* (**3**, **23**, **55**, **97**) by Kendyl Gibbons. Used with permission of author. "Practicing Humanism" (sermon) (**114**) by Kendyl Gibbons, 2002. Reprinted with permission of author.

GIBRAN   From "On Self-Knowledge" (**115**), in *The Prophet* by Kahlil Gibran, 1923.

GILBERT   "We Are All More Human Than Otherwise" (**98**) and "Beatitudes for Earth Sunday" (**147**), in *In the Holy Quiet of This Hour* by Richard Gilbert, 1995. *Building Your Own Theology 2: Exploring*, 2nd ed. (**129**) by Richard Gilbert, 2005. Reprinted with permission of author.

GOETHE   Selection (**116**) by Johann Wolfgang von Goethe, in *The Wisdom of Goethe* by John Stuart Blackie, 2004.

GOSPEL OF THOMAS   Gospel of Thomas, Saying 70 (**6**), trans. by Stevan Davies, 2002.

GOULD   "Telling Stories to the Seventh Generation: Resisting the Assimilationist Narrative of *Stiya*" (**72**) by Janice Gould, in *Reading Native American Women: Critical/Creative Representations* by Inés Hernández-Avila, 2004.

HAMER   Composite quotation (**27**), by Fannie Lou Hamer, in interview by Neil McMillen, Apr. 14, 1972, http://historymatters. gmu.edu/d/6918, and in *To the Mountaintop: Martin Luther King Jr.'s Mission to Save America: 1955–1968* by Stewart Burns, 2004.

HASSIDIC STORY   Hassidic story (**78**), retold by Doug Lipman. Reprinted with permission of author. For Doug's free storytelling newsletters, see www.StorytellingNewsletters.com.

HATHAWAY   *The Little Locksmith* (**100**) by Katherine Butler Hathaway, 1942.

HAY   From "Heresy Indeed" (**26**) in *This, My Letter* by Sara Henderson Hay, 1941. Reprinted with permission of the author's estate.

HENLY   "Invictus" (**105**) by William Earnest Henly, in *Americans' Favorite Poems: The Favorite Poems Project Anthology*, edited by Robert Pinsky and Maggie Dietz, 2000.

HESCHEL   *God in Search of Man: A Philosophy of Judaism* (**59**) by Abraham Joshua Heschel, 1976. *Between God and Man: An Interpretation of Judaism from the Writings of Abraham Joshua Heschel* (**77**) by Abraham Joshua Heschel, edited by Fritz A. Rothschild, 1959.

Hillel the Elder   Selection (**77**) by Hillel the Elder, in *The Life and Teachings of Hillel* by Yitzhak Buxbaum, 1994.

Holmes   Prayers (**19**, **36**) in *My Heart Leaps Up: A Lenten Manual* by Frank O. Holmes, 1986. Reprinted with permission of the author's estate.

Holmes   Selection (**20**) by John Haynes Holmes, in *A Summons Unto Men, an Anthology of the Writings of John Haynes Holmes,* edited by Carl Hermann Voss, 1971. Selection (**84**) by John Haynes Holmes, in *International Journal of Religious Education*, Vols. 16–17, 1939.

Hopedale declaration   Hopedale declaration (**92**), in *Recollections of a Varied Career* by William Franklin Draper, 1908.

Hopkins   "Pied Beauty" (**11**) by Gerard Manley Hopkins, in *Americans' Favorite Poems: The Favorite Poems Project Anthology*, edited by Robert Pinsky and Maggie Dietz, 2000. From "Inversnaid" (**131**) by Gerard Manley Hopkins, in *Poems* edited by Robert Bridges, 1918.

Isaiah   Isaiah 3:15 (**23**), New International Version.

Jewish Prayers   "A Prayer for Peace" (**79**) in *Gates of Prayer: The New Union Prayerbook* © 1975 Central Conference of American Rabbis and reprinted for use by permission of the CCAR. All rights reserved. Prayer (**80**), in *Mishkan T'filah: A Reform Siddur: Weekdays, Shabbat and Festivals*, edited by Elyse Frishman, 2007.

JOHN   John 15:12–13 (**91**), New Standard Revised Version. John 20:24–25 (**112**), English Standard Version.

JOHNSON   From "Lift Every Voice and Sing" (**87**) by James Weldon Johnson, in *African-American Poetry: An Anthology, 1773–1927,* edited by Joan R. Sherman, 1997.

JONES   Selection (**16**) by Elizabeth M. Jones, in *A Chosen Faith: An Introduction to Unitarian Universalism,* Rev. ed., by John A. Buehrens and Forrest Church, 1998.

KABIR   "If you want the truth . . ." (**123**) by Kabir, in *Kabir: Estatic Poems,* versions by Robert Bly, 2007.

KELLY   *A Testament of Devotion* (**4**) by Thomas R. Kelly, 1941.

KENDRICK   "Faith of a Unitarian Universalist Christian" (pamphlet) (**91**) by Stephen Kendrick, 2004.

KING   "Letter from Birmingham Jail" (**25**), in *Why We Can't Wait* by Martin Luther King Jr., 1963.

LANE   Chalice lighting (**137**) by Ed A. Lane. Reprinted with permission of author.

LAWRENCE   Selection (**14**) by D.H. Lawrence, in *The Selected Letters of D.H. Lawrence,* edited by James T. Boulton, 1997.

LEADING CLOUD   Selection (**130**) by Jenny Leading Cloud, in *Mankiller: A Chief and Her People* by Wilma Pearl Mankiller and Michael Wallis, 2000.

LERNER   "The State of the Spirit" (**18**) by Michael Lerner, in *Tikkun*, May/June 2002.

LOCKWOOD   *Grasshopper Dreaming: Reflections on Killing and Loving* (**138**) by Jeffrey A. Lockwood, 2002.

LUKE   Luke 10:25–37 (**57**), Luke 17: 20–21 (**83**), Luke 6:27–30 (**88**), Luke 6:31 (**90**), New Revised Standard Version.

LUTHER   Selection (**11**) by Martin Luther, in *Here I Stand: A Life of Martin Luther* by Roland H. Bainton, 1950.

LYONS   Address (**146**) by Oren Lyons, delivered to the United Nations in 1977, in *Native American Wisdom: A Spiritual Tradition at One with Nature*, edited by Alan Jacobs, 2008.

MALCOLM X   Address (**28**) by Malcolm X, delivered at the founding rally of the Organization of Afro-American Unity, March 8, 1964, in *By Any Means Necessary*, edited by George Breitman, 1970.

MANN   Address (**27**) by Horace Mann, delivered at Antioch College commencement, June 1859, in *American Education*, Vol. 16, 1912.

MARK   Mark 12:28–31 (**81**), New International Version.

MATTHEW   Matthew 26:50–52 (**31**), New International Version.

MAYER   Lyrics "Holy Now" (**9**) and "God Is a River" (**145**) by Peter Mayer. Reprinted with permission of author.

McKeeman   Prayer (**5**) by Gordon B. McKeeman. Reprinted with permission of author.

McTigue   Selection (**8**) by Kathleen McTigue in, *Everyday Spiritual Practice: Simple Pathways for Enriching Your Life*, edited by Scott W. Alexander, 1999. From "They Are With Us Still" (**33**) and from "New Year's Day" (**35**) by Kathleen McTigue. Reprinted with permission of author.

Micah   Micah 6:8 (**28**), New International Version.

Mishnah   Mishnah (**59**, **60**) in *Day by Day, Reflections on the Themes of the Torah from Literature, Philosophy and Religious Thought*, edited by Chaim Stern, 1998.

Montley   *In Nature's Honor* (**132**) by Pat Montley, 2005.

Mother Teresa   Brief quote (**91**), from p. 65, from *Something Beautiful for God: Mother Teresa of Calcutta* by Malcolm Muggeridge, copyright © 1971 by The Mother Teresa Committee. Reprinted by permission of HarperCollins Publishers. Mother Teresa's words © by the Mother Teresa Center, exclusive licensee throughout the world of the Missionaries of Charity for the works of Mother Teresa. Used with permission.

Muhammad   Selection (**66**) by Muhammad, in *A Brief History of the Fourteen Infallibles* by the World Organization for Islamic Services, 2001. Selection (**67**) by Muhammad, in *The Sayings of Muhammad,* trans. by Sir Abdullah Al-Mamun Suhrawardy, 1999.

MURFIN   "I Do Not Have a Personal Relationship With God" (**102**) by Patrick Murfin. Reprinted with permission of author.

NHAT HANH   *The Miracle of Mindfulness: An Introduction to the Practice of Meditation* (**7**) by Thich Nhat Hanh, trans. by Mobi Ho, 1975.

NICHOLS   *A Biblical Humanist Companion* (**81**) by John H. Nichols, 1989.

NOVAK   "Pray" (**117**) by Theresa Novak, in *With or Without Candlelight: A Meditation Anthology*, edited by Victoria Safford, 2009. Reprinted with permission of author.

OELBERG   "The Faith of a Unitarian Universalist Humanist" (pamphlet) (**106**, **116**) by Sarah Oelberg, 1996.

OWEN-TOWLE   *Freethinking Mystics With Hands* (**33**) by Tom Owen-Towle, 1998. "Welcome to Unitarian Universalism: A Community of Truth, Service, Holiness and Love" (pamphlet) (**101**) by Tom Owen-Towle, 1992.

P'ANG   Quote from p. 135 (Layman P'ang:12 l.) (**63**) by Layman P'ang, in *The Enlightened Heart: An Anthology of Sacred Poetry*, edited by Stephen Mitchell copyright © 1989 by Stephen Mitchell. Reprinted by permission of HarperCollins Publishers.

PARKER   *Blessing the World: What Can Save Us Now* (**15**, **34**, **121**) by Rebecca Parker, edited by Robert Hardies, 2006.

Parker   Prayer (**88**) by Theodore Parker, in *Prayers for Today*, edited by Herbert Vetter, 2004. "The Transient and Permanent in Christianity" (**92**) by Theodore Parker, in *Three Prophets of Religious Liberalism: Channing-Emerson-Parker*, 2nd ed., edited by Conrad Wright, 1986.

Patton   "Let Us Worship" (**3**), in *Services and Songs for the Celebration of Life* by Kenneth L. Patton, 1967. "The Way" (**115**) by Kenneth L. Patton. Reprinted with permission of Clarise E. Patton.

Peek   "A New Day" (**136**) by Anne Peek, in *For All That Is Our Life: A Meditation Anthology*, edited by Helen and Eugene Pickett, 2005. Reprinted with permission of author.

Pescan   From benediction (**32**) and from prayer (**37**) by Barbara Pescan. Reprinted with permission of author.

Psalm 131   Psalm 131 (**89**). Scripture taken from *The Message*. Copyright © 1993, 1994, 1995, 1996. Used by permission of NavPress Publishing Group.

Qur'an   Qur'an 30:19 (**65**), Qur'an 25:63 (**67**), and Qur'an 67:19 (**68**), in *Ayat Jamilah: Beautiful Signs: A Treasury of Islamic Wisdom for Children and Parents*, collected and adapted by Sarah Conover and Freda Crane, 2011. Qur'an 2:164 (**4**), Qur'an 49:13 (**65**), Qur'an 1:1–7 (**66**), and Qur'an 41:34–35 (**66**) trans. by Abdullah Yusuf Ali, 1934.

Rankin "Simple Pleasures" (**10**), "Palm Sunday" (**90**), and "Doubt" (**109**), in *Dancing in the Empty Spaces: Meditations* by David Rankin, 2001. Reprinted with permission of author.

Reeb Selection (**36**) by James Reeb, in *No Greater Love: The James Reeb Story* by Duncan Howlett, 1993.

Reeves Selection (**119**) by Gene Reeves. Reprinted with permission of author.

Rilke "Ich liebe meines Wesens…/I love the dark hours of my being" (**8**), in *Rilke's Book of Hours: Love Poems to God* by Rainer Maria Rilke, translated by Anita Barrows and Joanna Macy, copyright © 1996 Anita Barrows and Joanna Macy. Used by permission of Riverhead Books, an imprint of Penguin Group (USA) Inc.

Robinson Selection (**104**) by Christine Robinson. Reprinted with permission of author.

Robinson "Pain, Psalm, Prayer and a Promise" (**85**) by Ron Robinson, in *Christian Voices in Unitarian Universalism*, edited by Kathleen Rolenz, 2006.

Rohde "Poem in a Time of Peril" (**108**), in *In the Simple Morning Light* by Barbara Rohde, 1994. Reprinted with permission of author.

Rolenz Prayer for Justice Sunday (**40**) by Kathleen Rolenz. Reprinted with permission of author.

RUMI   "There is a life-force within your soul…" (**12**) by Jalal al-Din Rumi, trans. by Shahram Shiva. Reprinted with permission of Hohm Press, from *Rending the Veil*, 1995, www.hohmpress.com, Telephone: 800–381–2700. "Only Breath" (**70**) by Jalal al-Din Rumi, trans. by Coleman Barks with John Moyne, in *The Essential Rumi: New Expanded Edition*, edited by Coleman Barks, 2004. Reprinted with permission of Coleman Barks.

RYŌKAN   Qu. from Ryōkan {7 l.: "In all the ten directions of the universe, there is only one truth"/. . . ."} (**64**) from *The Gospel According to Jesus* by Stephen Mitchell, copyright © 1991 by Stephen Mitchell. Reprinted by permission of HarperCollins Publishers.

SAFFORD   From "Call to Worship" (**15**) and from "Desert Spring" (**94**), in *Walking Toward Morning: Meditations* by Victoria Safford, 2003. Reprinted with permission of author.

SALZBERG   *Faith: Trusting Your Own Deepest Experience* (**64**) by Sharon Salzberg, 2002.

SAMSON   "Can Humanism Be Religious?" (pamphlet) (**108**) by Peter Samson.

SCHULZ   Affirmation (**100**) by William F. Schulz. Reprinted with permission of author.

SCHWEITZER   Selection (**35**) by Albert Schweitzer, in *Singing the Living Tradition*, 1993. Selection (**134**) by Albert Schweitzer, in *Albert Schweitzer: An Anthology*, edited by Charles R. Joy, 1947.

SCOTT "Prophets" (**35**) by Clinton Lee Scott, in *Singing the Living Tradition*, 1993. From "Openness" (**120**), in *Promise of Spring: Forty Meditations* by Clinton Lee Scott, 1977.

SEN "Unto the Church Universal" (**49**) by Keshab Chandra Sen, arranged by John Haynes Holmes, in *Singing the Living Tradition*, 1993.

SHAFFER From "Were I to Teach a Course on God" (**14**) and "That Which Holds All" (**53**), in *Instructions in Joy: Meditations* by Nancy Shaffer, 2002. Reprinted with permission of author.

SHAKESPEARE *All's Well That Ends Well* (**106**) by William Shakespeare, 1623.

SHANTIDEVA From "The Way of the Bodhisattva" (**30**) by Shantideva, trans. by the Padmakara Translation Group, ©1997, 2006 by the Padmakara Translation Group. Reprinted by arrangement with Shambhala Publications Inc., Boston, MA. www.shambhala.com.

SHICK "My Saints" (**39**) in *Be the Change: Poems, Prayers and Meditations for Peacemakers and Justice Seekers* by Stephen Shick, 2009. Reprinted with permission of author.

SILKO "Landscape, History and the Pueblo Imagination" (**133**), in *Antaeus*, 57, Autumn 1986.

SIMCOX "A Mad Mix of Dedicated People" (**94**) by John Simcox, in *Christian Voices in Unitarian Universalism*, edited by Kathleen Rolenz, 2006.

SMITH   *A Quaker Book of Wisdom: Life Lessons in Simplicity, Service and Common Sense* (**23**, **100**) by Robert Lawrence Smith, 1998.

STARHAWK   *The Spiral Dance: A Rebirth of the Ancient Religion of the Great Goddess* (**130**) by Starhawk, 1999. *The Fifth Sacred Thing* (**139**) by Miriam (Starhawk) Simos © 1993 by Miram Simos. Used by permission of Bantam Books, a division of Random House, Inc. *Truth or Dare: Encounters with Power, Authority, and Mystery* (**143**) by Starhawk, 1987.

STEVENSON   Address (**51**) by Adlai Stevenson, in *A Chosen Faith: An Introduction to Unitarian Universalism*, Rev. ed., by John Buehrens and Forrest Church, 1998.

STRENG   Selection (**50**) by Frederick J. Streng in *A Chosen Faith: An Introduction to Unitarian Universalism*, Rev. ed., by John Buehrens and Forrest Church, 1998.

SUU KYI   "Freedom from Fear" (**40**), in *Freedom from Fear and Other Writings* by Aung San Suu Kyi, edited by Michael Aris, 1991.

SWIMME   "The Cosmic Creation Story" (**139**, **143**) by Brian Swimme, in *Readings in Ecology and Feminist Theology*, edited by Mary Heather MacKinnon and Moni McIntyre, 1995.

TAGORE   Selection (**16**) by Rabindranath Tagore, in *The Complete Poems of Rabindranath Tagore's Gitanjali: Texts and Critical Evaluation* by S.K. Paul, 2006. "The Religion of Man" (**69**) by Rabindranath Tagore, in *A Miscellany: Volume 3 of the English writings of Rabindranath Tagore* by Rabindranath Tagore and Sisir Kumar Das, edited by Sisir Kumar Das, 1996.

TENNYSON   From "The Higher Pantheism" (**86**) in *The Holy Grail and Other Poems* by Alfred Lord Tennyson, 1870.

TERESA OF AVILA   Selection (**25**) by Teresa of Avila, in *Entering the Castle: The Inner Path to God and Your Soul's Purpose* by Caroline Myss, 2007.

THOREAU   *Walden* (**17**) by Henry David Thoreau, 1854.

THURMAN   *Jesus and the Disinherited* (**25**) by Howard Thurman, 1949.

TILLICH   *The New Being* (**34**) by Paul Tillich, 1955.

TRAPP   "Each of the great religions" (**47**) by Jacob Trapp, in *A Chosen Faith: An Introduction to Unitarian Universalism*, Rev. ed., by John Buehrens and Forrest Church, 1998. Selections (**17**, **61**) in *The Light of a Thousand Suns* by Jacob Trapp, 1975.

TRUNGPA   *Cutting Through Spiritual Materialism* (**101**) by Chögyam Trungpa, 1973.

Tubman   "If you hear the dogs . . ." (**24**) attributed to Harriet Tubman, in *A People's History of Christianity: The Other Side of the Story* by Diana Butler Bass, 2009.

Tutu   Selection (**93**), in *God's Mission in the World: An Ecumenical Christian Study Guide on Global Poverty and the Millennium Development Goals*, Episcopal and Evangelical Lutheran Churches, 2006.

Tzu   "The ancients who followed Tao . . ." (**69**) by Lao Tzu, trans. by Stephen Addiss and Stanley Lombardo, in *Tao Te Ching*, © 1993 by Hackett Publishing Company, Inc. Reprinted by permission of Hackett Publishing Company, Inc. All rights reserved.

Ungar   "Boundaries" (**113**), in *Blessing the Bread: Meditations* by Lynn Ungar, 1996. Reprinted with permission of author.

Upanishad   Upanishad (**60**), in *Day by Day: Reflections on the Themes of the Torah from Literature, Philosophy and Religious Thought*, edited by Chaim Stern, 2000.

Walker-Riggs   Selection (**110**) by Judith Walker-Riggs. Reprinted with permission of author.

Walton   Selection (**111**) by Chris Walton. Reprinted with permission of author.

Wellemeyer   "Goddess Chant" (**140**), in *Admire the Moon* by Mary Wellemeyer, 2005. Reprinted with permission of author.

Weltner   Selection (**58**) by Linda R. Weltner, in "Discovering Unitarian Universalism from Catholic and Jewish Perspectives" (pamphlet) by Linda R. Weltner and Patrick T. O'Neill, 1995.

Wenzel   Selection (**32**) by H.G. Wenzel, in *A Chosen Faith: An Introduction to Unitarian Universalism*, Rev. ed., by John Buehrens and Forrest Church, 1998.

Weston   "Cherish Your Doubts" (**112**) by Robert T. Weston. Reprinted with permission of author.

Whitehead   *Dialogues of Alfred North Whitehead* (**104**) by Alfred North Whitehead, as recorded by Lucien Price, 1954.

Whitman   From "Song of Myself" (**130**), in *Leaves of Grass* by Walt Whitman, 1882.

Wikstrom   "An Old Friend" (**92**) by Erik Walker Wikstrom, in *Christian Voices in Unitarian Universalism*, edited by Kathleen Rolenz, 2006.

Willowroot   "Prayer of Becoming" (**144**) by Abby Willowroot. Reprinted with permission of author.

Wu-men   Quote from p. 47 (Wu-men: 4 l.) (**63**), from *The Enlightened Heart: An Anthology of Sacred Poetry*, edited by Stephen Mitchell copyright © 1989 by Stephen Mitchell. Reprinted by permission of HarperCollins Publishers.